OBJECT LESSONS

A book series about the hidden lives of ordinary things.

Series Editors:

Ian Bogost and Christopher Schaberg

Advisory Board:

Sara Ahmed, Jane Bennett, Jeffrey Jerome Cohen, Johanna Drucker, Raiford Guins, Graham Harman, renée hoogland, Pam Houston, Eileen Joy, Douglas Kahn, Daniel Miller, Esther Milne, Timothy Morton, Kathleen Stewart, Nigel Thrift, Rob Walker, Michele White

In association with

LOYOLA UNIVERSITY NEW ORLEANS

Georgia Tech Center for Media Studies

BOOKS IN THE SERIES

Bird by Erik Anderson
Blanket by Kara Thompson
Bookshelf by Lydia Pyne
Bread by Scott Cutler Shershow
Bulletproof Vest by Kenneth R. Rosen
Burger by Carol J. Adams
Cell Tower by Steven E. Jones
Cigarette Lighter by Jack Pendarvis
Coffee by Dinah Lenney
Compact Disc by Robert Barry
Doctor by Andrew Bomback
Driver's License by Meredith Castile
Drone by Adam Rothstein
Dust by Michael Marder
Earth by Jeffrey Jerome Cohen and Linda T. Elkins-Tanton
Egg by Nicole Walker
Email by Randy Malamud
Environment by Rolf Halden
Exit by Laura Waddell
Eye Chart by William Germano
Fake by Kati Stevens
Glass by John Garrison
Golf Ball by Harry Brown
Hair by Scott Lowe
Hashtag by Elizabeth Losh
High Heel by Summer Brennan
Hood by Alison Kinney
Hotel by Joanna Walsh
Jet Lag by Christopher J. Lee
Luggage by Susan Harlan
Magnet by Eva Barbarossa
Ocean by Steve Mentz
Password by Martin Paul Eve
Personal Stereo by Rebecca Tuhus-Dubrow
Phone Booth by Ariana Kelly

Pill by Robert Bennett
Political Sign by Tobias Carroll
Potato by Rebecca Earle
Questionnaire by Evan Kindley
Refrigerator by Jonathan Rees
Remote Control by Caetlin Benson-Allott
Rust by Jean-Michel Rabaté
Shipping Container by Craig Martin
Shopping Mall by Matthew Newton
Silence by John Biguenet
Sock by Kim Adrian
Souvenir by Rolf Potts
Snake by Erica Wright
Traffic by Paul Josephson
Tree by Matthew Battles
Tumor by Anna Leahy
Veil by Rafia Zakaria
Waste by Brian Thill
Whale Song by Margret Grebowicz
Bicycle by Jonathan Maskit (forthcoming)
Fat by Hanne Blank (forthcoming)
Fog by Stephen Sparks (forthcoming)
Football by Mark Yakich (forthcoming)
Gin by Shonna Milliken Humphrey (forthcoming)
Office by Sheila Liming (forthcoming)
OK by Michelle McSweeney (forthcoming)
Perfume by Megan Volpert (forthcoming)
Pixel by Ian Epstein (forthcoming)
Recipe by Lynn Z. Bloom (forthcoming)
Signature by Hunter Dukes (forthcoming)
Sticker by Henry Hoke (forthcoming)
Train by A. N. Devers (forthcoming)
TV by Susan Bordo (forthcoming)
Wheelchair by Christopher R Smit (forthcoming)

exit

LAURA WADDELL

BLOOMSBURY ACADEMIC
NEW YORK · LONDON · OXFORD · NEW DELHI · SYDNEY

BLOOMSBURY ACADEMIC
Bloomsbury Publishing Inc
1385 Broadway, New York, NY 10018, USA
50 Bedford Square, London, WC1B 3DP, UK

BLOOMSBURY, BLOOMSBURY ACADEMIC and the Diana logo are trademarks of
Bloomsbury Publishing Plc

First published in the United States of America 2020

Copyright © Laura Waddell, 2020

Cover design: Alice Marwick

For legal purposes the Acknowledgments on pp. 131–132 constitute an extension of this copyright page.

All rights reserved. No part of this publication may be reproduced or transmitted in any form or by any means, electronic or mechanical, including photocopying, recording, or any information storage or retrieval system, without prior permission in writing from the publishers.

Bloomsbury Publishing Inc does not have any control over, or responsibility for, any third-party websites referred to or in this book. All internet addresses given in this book were correct at the time of going to press. The author and publisher regret any inconvenience caused if addresses have changed or sites have ceased to exist, but can accept no responsibility for any such changes.

Library of Congress Cataloging-in-Publication Data
Names: Waddell, Laura, author.
Title: Exit / Laura Waddell.
Description: New York : Bloomsbury Academic, 2020. | Series: Object lessons| Includes bibliographical references and index.
Identifiers: LCCN 2020010167 | ISBN 9781501358159 (paperback) |
ISBN 9781501358142 (pdf) | ISBN 9781501358166 (ebook)
Subjects: LCSH: Farewells–Social aspects.
Classification: LCC GT3050 .W33 2020 | DDC 395–dc23
LC record available at https://lccn.loc.gov/2020010167

ISBN: PB: 978-1-5013-5815-9
ePDF: 978-1-5013-5814-2
eBook: 978-1-5013-5816-6

Series: Object Lessons

Typeset by Deanta Global Publishing Services, Chennai, India
Printed and bound in Great Britain

To find out more about our authors and books visit www.bloomsbury.com and sign up for our newsletters.

Dedicated to Rose, Ophelia, and Pepinot

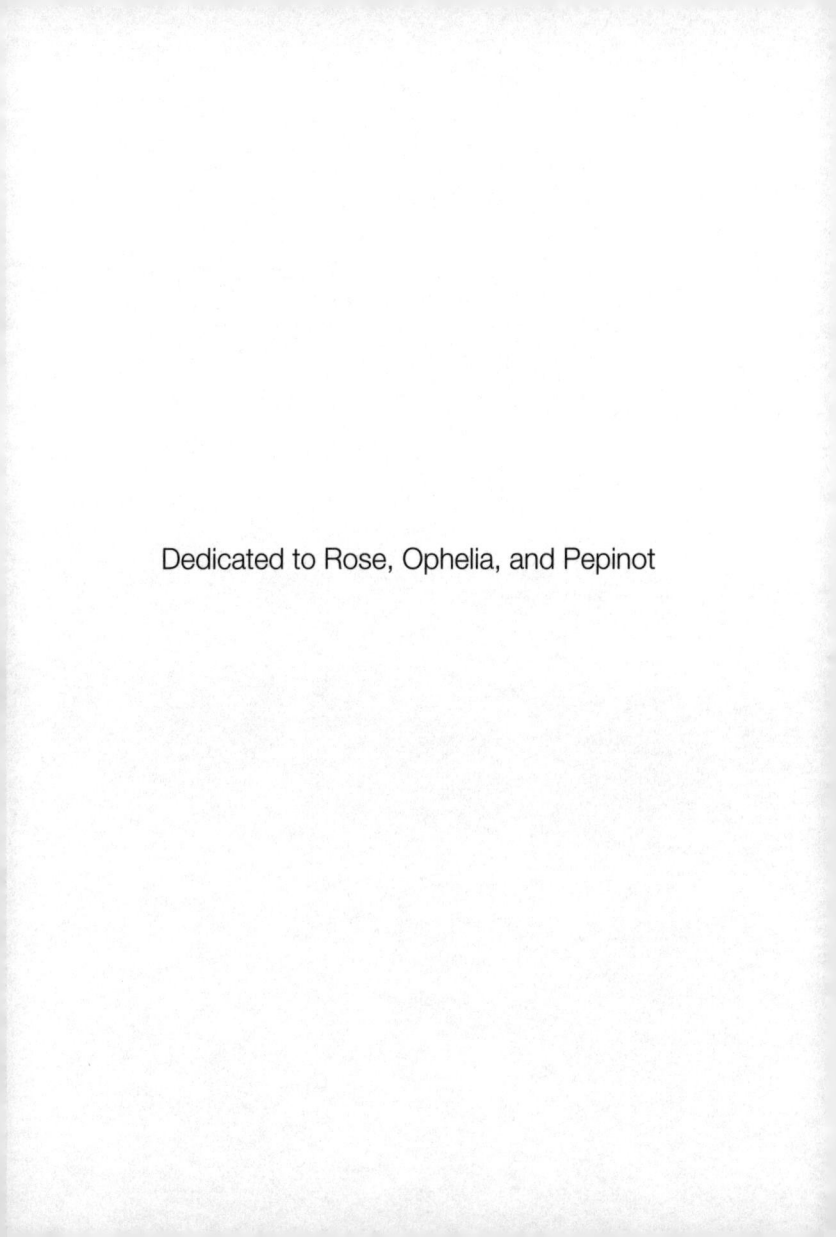

CONTENTS

Preface xiii

1 Words Associated with Exit 1

2 After the World of My Own Language Sank 9

3 Some Poet Throwing Forked Lightning 19

4a The History of Exit Signs 31

4b The Poetics of Exit Design 39

4c The Future of Exit Signs 55

5 Grouchland: Brexit, Sesame Street, and Garbage 67

6 Elevation 81

7 Evictions and Evacuations 95

8 Existential Exits 111

9 EXIT This Way 119

Acknowledgments 131
Notes 133
Index 144

PREFACE

Exit: a point between here and there, in or out.

An often subversive, only occasionally sign-posted dividing line between one thing and another. What happens when we cross over to the other side?

At one point in my early life I had a recurring dream of a small, dark, basement cabaret lounge. Other details were largely indistinct against black and velvety walls. There was maybe a wooden stool, and a small stage elevated one step above the floor. The slim suggestion of a bar in the back, but that's not important. Nobody else but me and my thoughts. If there was a performer, I was it, and the only audience member, too. (It's my subconscious, after all.) The most striking thing was a bright green exit sign, illuminated and blazing coolly, on the outside of the building instead of the inside, as though to go through the door was to exit one reality and enter another.

I don't have this neon green dream any longer, but I can still feel it; surreal and underground, like the jazz club I've never been to, or a performance art hot spot for those in the know. I came to the realization it probably represented my young idea of what a city might offer: mysterious places and nighttime pleasures with undefined edges. Like the fantasy metropolis after nightfall, the one I've never been to but visit in films. Shadowy, unknown, and requiring a bit of searching to find, full of potential to fall down the rabbit hole via basement shaft. A place where ideas might be allowed to probe weird corners; a metaphysical playground lit by nocturnal neon. It was the promise of adulthood before I could define illicit pleasures, only conjuring up elements of their atmosphere. And ultimately, it was something different: the projection of a future, far away, unlike any actuality I had a grasp on. I was striving for something. A form of performance, perhaps, or self-expression.

Later, I realized the exit sign as my nocturnal beacon was probably inspired by *Sesame Street*, where it features in a surprising number of musical numbers alongside countdowns and A-to-Z zaniness. To me, it all seemed to embody an urban coolness; American big cities far from my small town in Scotland, where numbers and letters and signs could run amok, and if I lived there, I might be part of it and play with them. Like the sign on a yellow taxi, four lit letters, it might take me somewhere. When I watched the episode of *Broad City* where Abby turns into Val, a slick singer in an eccentric, smoky cabaret, I felt a pang of recognition. Val is Abby's alter ego, who appears when she is black out drunk. In other words, the nightclub is a place she can only access when reality slips away. A fantasy self exists only in a fantasy place. It's probably just down the block from my exit sign room.

Since I've grown up, the exit signs I see on a daily basis are far more pedestrian than basement art joints of my childhood dreams, but they still hold transformative, subversive suggestion for me.

Glinting like a bottle of absinthe, there's something in the coming and going they signal that feels like flipping a card, taking a chance, moving on to the next thing (or place). Exits can be a series of small adventures, offering opportunities for impulse at each turn. It's the deliciousness of leaving an occasion early, slipping out without saying goodbye. Exit signs in the abstract make me think of the freedom to walk about; the freedom to leave and venture into something different. They turn me into a metaphysical flaneuse, walking the pathways of a dreamworld stocked with the fun functionality of the everyday world. But all of that suggests exiting on leisure time. A lot of the time, that's not the case. There are reasons for exits; we are propelled from as well as to something.

All around us are exits that mark the dividing line between being in one place or another. Being inside or outside. We're always on the move and so is the world around us, but if it feels like at any point we could come across an exit—like stepping into a black hole on the sidewalk and falling through it—exit signs are often there to guide the way. They mark the end of a movie experience after the credits have rolled, as the plush viewing space, with its feeling of being suspended in time while viewers are transported elsewhere, is swapped for the fresh air of the everyday world with its clockfaces, emails, and responsibilities. They mark the end of travel and arrival in a new place.

In charting the evolution of exit sign design and health and safety legislation, it's possible to see advances in citizen rights and how cities have grown in size and scale. Signs have a lot to do with our sense of place and security as we traverse the modern world. They say something about how we communicate, immediately and inaudibly, essential information that bridges languages and cultures. Exits direct flow on the streets, choreographing a pedestrian cha-cha-cha in opposite step to those entering—ways out that we take for granted but rely upon.

But exits are not always marked by signs. There are exits in politics, sports, video games, careers, sewage, poetry, relationships, reality, trash management, laundry cycles, mythology, electronics, music, sanity, water pipes, highways, coding, life, blood-letting, electric currents, ejaculation, squirting, exiting the scene of a crime, divorce, motorways . . .

. . . and only some of them clearly signal the dividing line between in or out, here or there. Exit signs are built into the architecture of our lives, present on every journey we have taken, every gig we have sung along to, every drink we've sipped over a breakup, always somewhere in the background, a beacon in the darkness, waiting to guide or force our next steps. Sometimes exits are a choice. Sometimes they are not.

There's a fine line between one reality and another, or between reality and surreality, and consequently how we conceive of ourselves. We push the revolving doors of *exit–entrance–exit* every day in many ways. Sometimes it frees us. But sometimes it sticks. Sometimes it is locked.

In writing this book, I came to better understand motion.
The kinetic energy of what pushes and pulls us.
Entrances and exits.
Exits and entrances.

1 WORDS ASSOCIATED WITH EXIT

I type in *words associated with exit*. I used to work for a British rival but a Google search puts an American dictionary at top, extracting info and auto-generating a box of text, intended to answer my question at first glance. Anyone culturally online is used to navigating varieties of English language not their own, and as I write this book for an editor in a different time zone, I take it in my stride. I am presented with the following words, grouped around bullet points like metal shavings to magnets. From these, I am meant to extrapolate meaning:

1. flight, retirement, retreat, running away, withdrawal.
2. diaspora, emigration, evacuation, exodus.
3. embarkation, embarkment.
4. disembarkation, egress.
5. abandonment, forsaking, relinquishment.

Emigration, but not immigration. That's despite embarkation and disembarkation, two opposites confidently taking up two bullet points. You get on a train, you get off a train. Either way you're going somewhere, unless there's a tree on the line. It's pretty much a continuous process, with the exit and the entrance mapped out on each side. Transportation that can be embarked or disembarked from pretty much always goes in a straight line, or between two easily definable points. Station to station. Port to port. A to B. Why do more complex journeys get fewer points, fewer words—don't we need all the help we can get to understand them?

At which point does emigration stop being an exit, and become an entrance? The algorithm is an extension of ourselves and our prejudices. It's materially different enough for us to deny its digital reflection on our faces. It is coding. We are flesh. But man built it. And like the dictionary, we are built into it. Its rules of form meet our conventions of usage and now our searches learn from us, trying to give us what is most useful, most saleable, most relevant. We get more of what we click on. Our opinions become serviced with complimentary information. There is no independent logic, no overarching rationale at play. Algorithms: they're just like us.

In an episode of the Twilight Zone *about journeying to Mars, that was the punchline. Aliens were frightening because they mirrored our worst human tendencies.*

The algorithm has decided emigration is a relevant answer, but immigration is not. Perhaps it is disinclined to include immigration as relevant to "exit" because so often our press and our politics focus on the numbers, dividing resources by people, dropping other details to the floor and kicking them to one side. Perhaps because much of what we see on tickertape or trending timelines can't encompass the meaning of any of those journeys (lives built or lost or made new or left out); and cannot comprehend that any entrance has been preceded by an exit predicated on a reason that exists in the minds of people in other places. That it is a process. That it is not, despite reports to the contrary, exclusively about us and our resources and our borders and our guns and our spaces and our places and our way of living and our cash and our Capitalism and our . . .? In, out. Us, them.

Not that it's necessary for "immigration" to be suffused with meaning palatable to you or me for it to be considered exit adjacent. Where there is an entrance, there is *always* an exit behind it of some shape, form, circumstance, locale, sentiment, or legal reality. It's tempting to point to those exits and "justify" them some way (he has exited Syria because of civil war; she has exited Germany to work in the English-language tuition sector) to make the entrance "legitimate," with the aim of countering xenophobic political ideas, but the exits exist either way. The point I'm trying to make is that we might only be witness to one side; we often forget the other. We see most clearly what is closest. But exits and entrances are dependent on each other for their meanings. So too, then, are immigration and emigration.

Of course, not every emigration/immigration has the neat resolution of entrance/exit, one on the other side of the other. (Not every disembarkation/embarkation does either. There were ten fatal airline accidents in 2018.) Purgatory exists in the form of migrant detention centers or, more rarely, denial of citizenship suspending an individual in legal limbo, neither here nor there. Exits are as likely to be as simple as they are long, tiring, frustrating, frustrated, and declined. And exits of one kind can be followed by exits of another.

As I write this chapter:

- the news tells me thirty-nine people from Vietnam were found deceased in the back of a freight truck in the south of England in autumn 2019[1]

- US Border Patrol reported 294 migrant deaths in the fiscal year 2017[2] (heat stroke, dehydration, hypothermia)

- according to the UN, 4,503 migrants died across the world in 2018[3] (mostly in the Mediterranean Sea)

- San Diego–based Border Angels estimate over 10,000 deaths have occurred across the US-Mexico border since 1994[4]

- the Missing Migrants Project, which "tracks deaths of migrants, including refugees and asylum-seekers, who have gone missing along mixed migration routes worldwide," has a count surpassing 60,000 over the last two decades. (A footnote on the website's "about" page notes that "the views expressed do not necessarily reflect the Government of the United Kingdom's official policies.")[5]

- and on the day I stop writing and send in this manuscript, a UN study has revealed the US has the highest number of children in immigration-related detention, at over 100,000.[6]

These are some numbers associated with Exit. And there have been cases of individuals charged and prosecuted under federal law, for the misdemeanor of entering private land without permit, while leaving water in Arizona for anyone crossing the land under triple-digit Fahrenheit temperatures.

Immigrants are lumped together in an ideological category encompassing those who arrive, contemplate arriving, may one day contemplate arriving, or who never arrive but seep into the political consciousness as abstract figures, the reasoning underpinning domestic politics, distribution of resources, and the amping up of nationalist militarist rhetoric. Immigrants and asylum seekers are lumped together clumsily. They are carefully kept away, however, from discussions on weapon sales and war.

The algorithm is in denial. We are to believe exits and entrances have nothing to do with one another, that the only duo is legal/illegal. Tickets are printed, and with them recipient citizens come and go, cross borders, come back. Others, who are considered to have appeared suddenly, as though out of thin air, we deny they have been on any kind of journey at all.

In the 2017 book *Tell Me How It Ends*,[7] author Valeria Luiselli reflects on her experience as volunteer translator for unaccompanied children reaching the US–Mexico border. Questions asked of migrant children after arduous travel build their case to stay. The process, full of gaps to fall between for anyone not least the small, stretches too thin the volunteers and charities providing legal and other services. Try as they might, they cannot meet demand. Children answer box-ticking questions that will determine their fate with lack of comprehension, fear, and nonlinear answers. They are so young. Their journeys have had confusing beginnings, middles, and ends.

I once stood for a long time before an exhibition of the photographs of Sergey Ponomarev, documenting boats reaching shore and trains packed tightly with people. Unusually, he gets close enough to see fatigue upon individual faces. I was unable to look away from the direct gazes of people waiting wearily in a long registration line, herded by Slovenian police. How often do we look need right in the eye? Petty frustrations are my only frame of reference; timetabled travel gone awry. Delays. Perhaps we need to bear witness to each stage of the journey in order to understand it better. To see that immigration is emigration. To see that exits are entrances, and vice versa, and that everything is linked by long, fine threads across the world. But I realize the problem isn't logic. The algorithm runs on something else.

I close the tab with the search results. I scroll down my timeline. I see a tweet from immigration attorney Bridget Cambria reading: "Longest child in family detention is MSHS, age 6. She's been in immigration detention for 128 days. She was a spider for Halloween. Last night she sat in a corner in the Berks babyjail and cried to be reunited with both her mom and dad. #endfamilydetention #freetheBerkskids."[8]

Followed by "We sat with her tonight to braid her hair. Her fav. animal is a rabbit. She misses her puppy. She wants to be a vet. When she leaves jail she wants the biggest pizza she can find. There's really good pizza in NJ—where her mom is waiting. She likes pineapple on her pizza."[9] and "BTW—it's the longest child in family detention in the entire US—if it wasn't clear. We only do this in Pennsylvania. Their family could be reunited instantly, if immigration would choose to. Like tomorrow. It's ICEs discretion to keep her locked up. Her case is just pending."[10]

There is a petition. Online support is gathering around this child who has not seen her mother for six months. I hope her case is resolved; I go back to check for updates. I hope that an entrance follows her exit, that no part of her is denied. And this is only one of many children, many of whom have no legal support. Words related to exit: abandonment.

I have realized I am always certain of the destination on my ticket. Other than disaster, I trust my exits will be followed by entrances. This girl is at this moment the longest detained, but it is an ongoing story; the days detained get longer every day.

2 AFTER THE WORLD OF MY OWN LANGUAGE SANK

Art, for its ability to humanize, to provoke empathy, and generally to communicate ideas between one person and another, has been a focus of fascist regimes throughout history.

- diaspora, emigration, evacuation, exodus.

These words linked to exit which speak of necessity and question the possibility of choice. That tell a story, accidentally, in their algorithmic grouping. Exit as forced, and widespread, and dangerous, and depleting. Exit as all of these things at once.

The cultural policy of the Nazis was the remit of Joseph Goebbels, who had the responsibility of scrutinizing many forms of art and media and found creative opportunities for cruelty in the task. In the autumn of 1933, it became mandatory for creators across art, film, books, music and more, or anyone who sold art, to become a member of the Reichskulturkammer (Reich Culture Chamber). This was a way for the Nazis to control artistic and media output, promoting classical aesthetics inspired by the Greeks and Romans that were considered instructive to the Aryan ideal, and banishing anything else. Among other things, they disallowed surrealism and Dada, Jewish music, and the blues. Trading was banned for anyone on the outside. Artists without membership could not exhibit their work and were cut off from materials. But worse even than being prevented from working was that those who did not register—or more accurately, weren't permitted to register—were labelled degenerate. It was not long before this developed along explicitly anti-Semitic lines, as had always been the underlying aim.

"From May 1935, the right to membership also required proof of Aryan ancestry. However, artists such as Ernst Blensdorf who was neither Jewish nor had a Jewish background nor was a member of a political party were also rejected. This shows that all artists whose work did not confirm to the National Socialist ideologies risked rejection and subsequent persecution."[1]

The intention was to depict these artists as outsiders, not only where their racial and religious heritage overlapped with the Reich's program of widespread persecution, but for their ideas. They were held up as examples; entire movements cut off from peers and collaborators. A fascist regime will always view ideas, even when not explicitly political but those which are artistic, creative, and so open to interpretation, as a threat. Fascist regimes depend on unity of thought, or submission to it. Art lifts the spirits too much for that. It teaches us about ourselves and takes us out of ourselves. It carries us to unexpected places and possibilities, questioning the everyday. None of this is palatable to regimes requiring unified ideology and eugenic control.

The situation worsened. The cruelty of exclusion degraded further into punishment. In 1937, Munich was host to the *Degenerate Art Exhibition*, which showcased the work of artists barred from the Reichskulturkammer. By making an example of intellectuals and artists, a threat looms for other citizens. Do not to stray too far into self-expression, or you will be considered an outsider. Be with us on the inside or cast out of society completely. Artists, of course, were only one segment among the Jewish and other populations persecuted as a whole. But by exhibiting work considered unsuitable, the Nazi regime warned onlookers off engaging with those considered undesirable, or they too might face consequences. Others scrutinized were artists who were married to Jews, those suspected linked to the Communist Party, and those whose paintings differed from the Aryan ideal.

A year later, an exhibition in Britain attempted to repatriate the reputations of emigre artists decried as Degenerates in their home country but who had subsequently and hastily fled for their safety, now beyond reach of repercussions from the Reich. The *Exhibition of Twentieth Century German Art* took place in New Burlington Galleries, in London, in 1938.

"The 269 exhibits executed in various styles; Expressionism was represented by Paula Modersohn Becker and Ludwig Kirchner, the Bauhaus by Oskar Schlemmer, Surrealism by Max Ernst and political art of the New Sachlichkeit and Dada by Otto Dix and George Groscz."[2]

But in an atmosphere of looming war, responses were muted, with the critic Raymond Mortimer going so far as to comment, "people who go to see the exhibition are only too likely to say: if Hitler doesn't like these pictures, it's the best thing about Hitler."[3]

What Happens in the Art of Those Cast out, Persecuted, and Othered?

Displacement is a running motif in the works of writer Stefan Zweig. It is always there: a sense of being external to one's surroundings, and far from what one would consider home. The feeling that home, and peace of mind, is always somewhere else, with a door closed to re-entering.

Zweig was born in Vienna in 1881, the son to a Jewish textile merchant and banking heiress. His reputation as a writer on Jewish cultural questions and of fiction quickly grew, and his acclaim was considerable across Europe and in America, where he later settled, having first moved to England before the advance of German troops through Europe sent him and his wife further westward. Like the exhibition of Degenerate Artists that pointed to outsiders as threats to Germany, Zweig's books were burned in a campaign called *Action Against the Un-German Spirit*.

Others whose work was targeted included Hesse, Freud, and Brecht. The pioneering *Institut für Sexualwissenschaft* [Institute of Sex Research], which developed understanding of and campaigned for equality for LGBT peoples, underwent a particularly crushing loss of studies and archives in the fires. Its founder Magnus Hirschfeld was a particular target for being both Jewish and gay and a prominent intellectual. He continued to write in exile. "I shall be glad and grateful if I can spend some few years of peace and repose in France and Paris, and still more grateful to be enabled to repay the hospitality accorded to me, by making available those abundant stores of knowledge acquired throughout my career."[4]

Many scenes of Zweig's novels take place in transient, temporary places where humans are passing through but not staying indefinitely, such as train carriages and hotels. There are near misses at stations, conversations with lovers delayed by the sluggish rhythm of postal services, and uncomfortable, dismayed emotions left lingering in lobbies and station terminals. His books are permeated with a sense of loss, for lives that may have been lived differently, and are as eerie as they are moving. He also wrote a biography of Mary Queen of Scots, who was imprisoned for ten years of her life, and who straddled national identities uncomfortably, having grown up and grown accustomed to high society in France before returning to take the throne in an unfamiliar Scotland and ultimately falling prey to displacement plots and hostile machinations.

Chess Story,[5] also known as *The Royal Game*, is a short, sharp thriller a little different from most of Zweig's work. Rather than his habitual themes of displacement, discomfort, being where one doesn't want to be, and the impersonal nature of hotels simmering throughout the plot, these things are brought into sharp focus and to the fore. A man is taken political prisoner in a reasonably comfortable hotel; for the duration, he is confined to his room. Quickly it becomes a mental as well as physical prison. By chance and daring, the man gets hold of a book on the rules of chess and obsessively consumes it, fantasizing of faux games and developing detailed strategy. The devotion with which he pursues the game takes the form of mania, but it is also a mental escape from the unchanging landscape, and ultimately his salvation. His mind has escaped the conditions placed on his body; through it he finds an exit and travels beyond the guarded door.

Zweig's contemporary, Irmgard Keun, also wrote explicitly of displacement. After a failed bid to join the Reichschriftumskammer—the author's association of Nazi Germany set up in the same way as the Artist's Association—Keun was banned from publishing new work and suffered a loss of income. She went into exile, landing in Belgium and the Netherlands, but later returned to Germany using a pseudonym. Her biography is surprising, daring, and patchy in places of frequent moving and the occasional requirement to conceal identity. It was reported she died by suicide in Amsterdam. In an interview, Keun's daughter, Martina Keun-Geburtig, answers the question if her mother was a happy woman, "Well, she always said that the Nazis took her best years. Starting in 1933 her success was abruptly ended through the book-burning up until '45, '46. It's a pretty long time…"[6]

Keun's book *Child of All Nations*[7] is told through the eyes of a young girl whose father is a political journalist. It is unsafe for them to continue living in Germany and the family moves for fear of their lives. Like Zweig, Keun often chose hotels as her setting. The young girl narrator struggles to understand why the family moves from place to place. With an innocent's eye, she is able to depict the loss of humanity in simple terms and capture its impact on everyday life, while only vaguely being aware of the names Hitler and Mussolini. Her father cannot come to terms with his work being banned. Like other writers at risk of persecution, art and writing appears in Keun's work as symbols of freedom. To prevent it is to restrict expression: willful and targeted cultural vandalism in an attempt to suppress and persecute citizens pushed out of German society.

Recently Zweig's work has seen a resurgence in interest after republication of a few attractively packaged editions, and the filmmaker Wes Anderson taking elements of his work, very slightly, as inspiration for his highly stylized caper *The Grand Budapest Hotel*. There has also been contention in critical circles as to his quality. In critic Michael Hofman's opinion, "Zweig just tastes fake. He's the Pepsi of Austrian writing." Even the author's suicide note, Hofmann suggests, causes one to feel "the irritable rise of boredom halfway through it, and the sense that he doesn't mean it, his heart isn't in it (not even in his suicide)."[8]

In delivering his themes, Zweig often constructed romantic plot lines, running with currents of insecurity and anxiety. There are many clubs, literary and otherwise, leery of anything coded feminine. Members self-refer and mutually affirm through ritualistic scorn of outsiders. (Women writers know this.)

Zweig confronted death and loss. He did not just live it; he wrote it. It haunts his work. His prose was silky and at times sentimental, but he was the Coca-Cola, the real deal. His gift as a writer was shaped always by the extraordinary pressures on his life, fleeing ethnic genocide and ever after in exile. His books impart something of the perpetual sensation of being an outsider, external always, to one's surroundings.

"I was sure in my heart from the first of my identity as a citizen of the world,"[9] reads a line from Zweig's autobiography. Such a statement is a desire to belong. It's a world where there are no borders, no endless exile. But he never found a way back in. Having exited, through force, he could never re-enter.

Then there is the last piece of Zweig's writing. It is his suicide note, left behind in Brazil in 1942, where Zweig and his second wife (who died in tandem with him) had travelled on to.

"Every day I learned to love this country more, and I would not have asked to rebuild my life in any other place after the world of my own language sank and was lost to me and my spiritual homeland, Europe, destroyed itself.

But to start everything anew after a man's 60th year requires special powers, and my own power has been expended after years of wandering homeless. I thus prefer to end my life at the right time, upright, as a man for whom cultural work has always been his purest happiness and personal freedom – the most precious of possessions on this earth.

I send greetings to all of my friends: May they live to see the dawn after this long night. I, who am most impatient, go before them."[10]

Exit as endless, perpetual, fatal. Exit felt to the bones. It falls to us, left behind, to observe.

3 SOME POET THROWING FORKED LIGHTNING

Exit: to be on the outside, to opt out, to leave in search of something else

Once, in my day job as a publisher, I had a conversation with a writer who had written her first book in many years in the Scots language. She told me that after years of being stuck in English, she tried writing in her other language, and to her surprise, the words flowed.

After the Acts of Union of 1707, which formed the modern United Kingdom, English superseded Scots as the official language used in schools and in written correspondence. (Critics of Scots' status as a language often point to a lack of written standardization as "proof.") Some writers and thinkers began moving in circles that considered Scots brash and lower class, and elocution lessons promoted Anglicized pronunciations. This happened prior to Robert Burns becoming prominent as Scotland's best-known poet—

his work resisted the rejection of Scots language in literary circles at a time a lingual split was forming between working-class and wealthier Scots.

A tension developed between inside and outside worlds. Scots spoken in the household was stored there, with speakers switching to English for bureaucracy, politics, professions, and schooling. As recently as 1946, a report from the Scottish Education Department considered Scots "not the language of 'educated' people anywhere, and could not be described as a suitable medium of education or culture."[1] Some today would not disagree; shame persists.

A majority of Scottish citizens now speak English as their first tongue, but are familiar with Scots to some degree, or speak a hybrid called Scots-English with its distinct grammatical patterns. Many of us with access to dual languages write in English because it is how we were taught to write and because we always have. Some singers shed their everyday accents for the Anglicized-American dominant in our pop culture.

In recent decades, there has been a sharper understanding of how minority and indigenous languages and cultures all over the world can be suppressed, and subsequent impacts on freedom of expression. The preservation of Scots flares up in waves of political and cultural trends; funding is directed to its teaching, publishing, and broadcasting. The same is true with Gaelic, distinct from Scots, often sidelined as even more minor. Now, the Scottish Parliament and other official bodies make information available in Scots alongside the many other languages spoken here, which include Arabic and Polish.

> But what remains of this difficult history, of dual languages and identities duelling? Perhaps in coming to terms with a forced exit, we continue to let parts of ourselves be cast out by ourselves, some scripts lost in bottles, undeciphered at sea.

Most of my Scots words came from my grandfather, who I called Papa, and who spoke them in the house I grew up in. My favorite word he used is "snawplough." That's snowplow in translation. Both syllables are given equal emphasis, and "snaw" is pronounced like the first three letters of "snot." Two soft syllables for the soft stuff that is cleared away. A foot rises, a foot falls; the path grows a little clearer. Snawplough isn't in my own vocabulary as a speaker, although I understand it as a listener and a reader.

There are similarities in the linguistic makeup of Scotland and Ireland, and Irish writer Eimear McBride has said that a multitude of languages probably contributed to the acclaimed experimentation of Irish writing. "It forms my understanding of language—that impertinence that the Irish have with the language."[2]

Researcher Sue Rainsford elaborates on this idea, describing McBride's use of language as

> the fusion of a visceral, articulate ferocity with an implicit, expansive feminism. Her protagonists are women and girls

governed by the vulgar and the brutal, the unforgiven and unforgivable, and this incarnate modernism works to make visible a fuller spectrum of their experience. Disallowing easy prescriptions of "*destructive*" and "demeaning," they pursue pleasure and selfhood and achieve, if not selfhood itself, a kind of transcendence that lifts them beyond the grasp of societal norms. Ultimately, it is McBride's artful transcribing of pleasure and pain, those moments that see the body become porous and "speak itself," that grants the female body and psyche their full reign with nuances, confusions, and revelations intact.[3]

Like snawplough, I sometimes wonder what else has exited my tongue and pen. What has been lost in the storm.

In the book *White*, a theory of the color, designer Kenya Hara goes in search of "whiteness" in Japanese culture, examining its use in book design, its presence in nature, and just as white is an absence of color, the meanings found in other absences such as gaps in conversation. He describes the feeling that things are becoming semi transparent—building, people, words:

> Architecture feels lighter because of its use of glass and other new building materials, while the words that traverse the net float about in limbo with no real place to call home…
> […] We struggle on day after day, attempting to expand the freshness and the promise we feel in this new reality. After all, this semitransparent world is likely to go on growing.

Perhaps the greater part of our conscious minds will end up residing there. Yet the snow keeps falling. Flakes silently dance down to rest in my palm, where they melt into drops of light. White still has the power to bestow its divine grace upon these bodies of ours, which can neither disappear, nor renew themselves, nor turn semi-transparent. It looks like the snow will go on falling for a while.[4]

What are exits, if not turning away from the color and clutter of one situation into another whose possibility and potential is yet to come? A blank canvas; the space to create. Although sometimes that's frightening, too.

Helen Adam was a Glasgow-born poet who reported that, not until she left Scotland and moved to America in the late 1930s, was she able to find her poetic voice. She found her groove in performing traditional Scots ballads, an oral rather than written tradition and so by its nature tenuously recorded in history, mixing with the San Francisco Beats scene as it flourished in the 1950s. Fellow poet Edwin Morgan described the effect of her move as a jolt bringing to the surface what was already there:[5]

Although she had grown up in a literary household and been in college when Hugh MacDiarmid was asserting the political necessity of claiming Scottish literature and dialect as distinctly separate from English, all the poems Adam had written while she lived in the UK followed English rules and dictionaries It was not until she got to America that she began investigating her own native Scots language and incorporating Lallan dialect into her ballads. Similarly, Ginsberg encouraged his students at Naropa Institute, on a day when they were studying Helen Adam and the ballad tradition, to remain true to their own regional American dialects.[6]

I can imagine Adam testing her sense of self. Leaning into the differences between her voice and others, as well as bringing something new and different to the linguistic scene. Her ballads were hearty songs full of mythmaking, and her lyrical voice was pulled along by their bounding beat. They were lustful and intemperate, eerie and portentous, and sometimes humorous. She was inspired by an "extraordinary unearthly quality in the lonely places, in the moors and glens"[7] of her home country, and also the Romantics which came before her, telling stories of wildness and women.

> The bonds of being dissolved and broke.
> Her body she dropped like a cast off cloak.
> Her shackled soul to its kindred sped.
> In devouring lust with the wolves she fled.
> —The Fair Young Wife[8]

In the words of Prevallet,

> Adam's subversion of traditional forms [...] revises traditional content with regard to gender. In most ballads,

women, no matter how strong, are rarely positioned outside of domestic space. Even if they are travelling, they are still traversing a passage between one form of bond to another. In Adams' *ballads* […] women are active protagonists. They are the ones who seek out their rights of passage, even if they are aided by supernatural powers.[9]

It took exiting Scotland for Adam to feel able to engage with the Scots language, experimenting and self-reflecting, and most of all rummaging through language in its varying forms, with the belief there was truth to find in words.

> Let words be naked
> As Yeats said, walking
> The streets unashamed.
> Let the boast and chatter
> Of shop and office
> Somehow disclose,
> Through some poet throwing
> Forked lightning
> The essential secret
> All language hides.[10]

What have I exited, in order to write? What have I removed myself from in order to feed the impulse to spend time tucked away with books and thoughts and what I might make with them?

Places, spaces, people, stretching back always.

Recently, the internet. My tendency to spend a long time scrolling down its timelines, a little like falling down a ladder. Each rung, a news story, something depressing, something or someone antagonistic. Lovely things, too. But all noise I had to shut out in order to write. I have exited tabs and exited applications, technically and mentally (although the feeling takes a while to dissipate). I have killed off my digital selves entirely in order to concentrate, lacking the willpower to just not look. I cannot do both. I cannot find the peace of mind required to think while my body still jumps to the endlessly refreshing stimulus. I know all the benefits: online turned real friends, community, networking, but I also understand it is a form of mental labor I have taken on without really realizing it, following the small bursts of dopamine it offers like breadcrumbs.

With the temporary exit from social media I have temporarily exited everyday habits. The habit lurks in drop-down menus and sites in my history. The breaks I take in between work activities which I so often spend, unthinkingly keying in the first letter, refreshing the same few sites. T is for Twitter. My impulse to check every five, ten, twenty minutes, and the vague, pervasive anxiety that arises when I don't. Just in case. In case what? I have to reply to a question as yet unasked? I have to justify myself by performing myself? I must continue the capitalist project of self-branding? Yet I feel no less anxious when I give in and look. It's what I do before sleep and the opening act for dreams. A habit, like a bell ringing, that I struggle to ignore if I don't entirely silence it by throwing it out of the window. It's only by contrast I realize my ears have been ringing all this time.

Hara says, "Even had the invention of paper followed the development of electronic technology, I am convinced that the sheer act of holding a sheet of paper, so full of creative possibility, would bring about a surge of human imagination."[11]

Sometimes the feeling of entering is the feeling of exiting other situations. Let me be clearer: I have entered situations, rooms, and mental states in order to pursue writing just as I have exited situations, rooms, and mental states in order to pursue writing. The same is true for my general well-being. There are right turns and wrong turns. Unexpected turns and subconscious turns. Sometimes roads are blocked and doors locked.

With social media, I had something to exit in the first place because I wanted to be in the midst of it all. Sometimes what we gravitate toward is not what we really want, but its mirage.

To write this book I had to follow exit signs.

I unlearned the cannon. I don't mean I threw it all out. But it was by working in publishing and seeing how commerce shapes what ends up on shelves, and the pitfalls of critical clique, and realizing that I had spent my student years reading, overwhelmingly, writers who were financially comfortable white men—only after that did I see a need to proactively seek out other things to read. Sometimes led by taste, sometimes with a desire to just read something different. I fell down rabbit holes with increasing delight. Who knew? The self-confidence to question what is ingrained by repetition through centuries can take its own time to develop.

When is holding a book not holding a book? This is not a riddle.

I have met readers who say they are "not real readers" because they don't think their interest is serious enough to claim the title. The same is true for not-writers who can't reconcile writing in and of their own environments with historically esteemed books. Yet I have known a few publishers, the *makers* of books, who themselves read less frequently for pleasure than these not-readers. Certain studies show that women readers will read across gender pretty evenly, but men are much more likely to gravitate to books by other men. Boys are less likely to be encouraged to read in the classroom and at home. Children in low-income households have more limited access to books. Libraries are closing down everywhere and illiteracy is still widespread. When people perceive themselves as outsiders to "reading" they are usually uncertain about the snobbery that exists around education and books, recalling the foreboding rights and wrongs of reading in class, and the persisting historical association of books for the learned and elite. "Not real readers" are uncertain about the right they have to place personal judgement on a book, on art generally, on ravens and writing desks.

There are rooms plastered in exit signs, where the sound of silence is only the forewarning of alarms going off.

I modelled my inner life as a hormonal teenager on Anaïs Nin's excessiveness. In her writing, sensuality gushes everywhere, spilling over. Rolling in velvet in one sentence, eating lemons the next. Excess in all things, every nerve rubbed raw.

Online, Nin still attracts curious onlookers, prone to their own extremes of feeling. The titles of her erotic books are snapped up as subversive pseudonyms on every platform where users remake themselves as they see fit. As a midcentury woman, she had darker concerns and mores, too, only partially reflecting the social standards of the day. Her racial exoticism is bitter tasting; forays after fetish chase taboos into the darkest of corners. She had her own misfortunes. A then-illegal abortion is described in oblique terms in her book *Incest*. She experienced abuse. One of the saddest moments in her diaries is her concern that orgasm encouraged pregnancy, and so she held back from "radius and rainbows."[12]

A misfit maximalist with a penchant for masochism. An outsider, an outlier. She very often describes compulsion to scoop up all pleasure a lifetime could offer. "I want to kneel as it falls over me like rain, gather it up with lace and silk, and press it over myself again,"[13] she said of happiness.

Anaïs the sensualist, Anaïs the fantasist. And to what end?

"Had I not created my whole world, I would certainly have died in other people's."[14]

I began to wonder if my own desire to go somewhere— away, outside, apart— was as much about slipping away from constrictions as it was a search for the space I needed to write. A mental exiting of macho-capitalist structures of esteem and external validation, climbing out of my assigned square in its grid as a young Scottish working-class woman writer, in order to breathe, to live, to self-actualize creatively and follow my intuition.

4a THE HISTORY OF EXIT SIGNS

The Fire

In the development of exit signs, we can read social history.

On the chilly Saturday afternoon of March 25, 1911, the Triangle Shirt Waist Company in Greenwich Village in Manhattan caught on fire just as shifts were ending. The workers, mostly immigrant women from Italian or Jewish backgrounds, were starting to think of heading home. It was the last day of long week of work, with Sundays off, and $7 to $12 weekly wages.

The source: a vast waste bin, full of fabric cuttings accumulated over a couple of months, suddenly bursting into flames. It was never discovered why; speculation ranges from a cigarette snuck in by one of the cutters, flouting the ban on smoking to while away the shift, to sparks from industrial machinery packed among reams of highly flammable fabric. The shirtwaists, a kind of tailored blouse, were popular with working-class women for the greater range of movement they afforded than dresses.

It wouldn't have been the first time arson was used as an insurance fraud in the garment industry, but that day the owners happened to be in the building along with their children, perhaps dropping in between weekend activities.

A passerby, on spotting smoke billowing from the eighth floor of the tall building, the bottom of the three levels the factory operated on, including the ninth and tenth, alerted the authorities. Meanwhile, a worker on the eighth floor telephoned to the tenth floor to warn them of the fire, but there was no telephone line on the ninth, and neither was there any kind of fire alarm. Workers tried to escape from encroaching flames but quickly discovered exits were locked.

The factory owners were in the habit of locking the doors to prevent the possibility of their workers stealing from them, with women's purses inspected on their way out. Some workers piled in an elevator and safely made it to the roof. Two elevator operators made journeys up and down three times, retrieving people from the fire-stricken ninth floor, but were forced to stop the rescue operation when heat pressure became too much for the warping elevator mechanism. Some of those waiting jumped desperately into the shaft, attempting to climb cables.

On the outside, the fire brigade had arrived. But with floors on fire higher than the reach of their ladders, there was little they could do. The iron fire escape, which had been built (with city permission) instead of a typical third staircase, collapsed to the ground with twenty workers on it, who died after a drop of 100 feet. Bystanders saw workers jump to their deaths from the windows. Many others were stuck inside, behind the locked doors.

Louis Waldman, later a New York Socialist state assemblyman, described the scene years later:

> One Saturday afternoon in March of that year—March 25, to be precise—I was sitting at one of the reading tables in the old Astor Library. It was a raw, unpleasant day and the comfortable reading room seemed a delightful place to spend the remaining few hours until the library closed. I was deeply engrossed in my book when I became aware of fire engines racing past the building. By this time I was sufficiently Americanized to be fascinated by the sound of fire engines. Along with several others in the library, I ran out to see what was happening, and followed crowds of people to the scene of the fire.
>
> A few blocks away, the Asch Building at the corner of Washington Place and Greene Street was ablaze. When we arrived at the scene, the police had thrown up a cordon around the area and the firemen were helplessly fighting the blaze. The eighth, ninth, and tenth stories of the building were now an enormous roaring cornice of flames.[1]

Word had spread through the East Side, by some magic of terror, that the plant of the Triangle Waist Company was on fire and that several hundred workers were trapped. Horrified and helpless, the crowds—I among them—looked up at the burning building, saw girl after girl appear at the reddened windows, pause for a terrified moment, and then leap to the pavement below, to land as mangled, bloody pulp. This went on for what seemed a ghastly eternity. Occasionally a girl who had hesitated too long was licked by pursuing flames and, screaming with clothing and hair ablaze, plunged like a living torch to the street. Life nets held by the firemen were torn by the impact of the falling bodies. The emotions of the crowd were indescribable. Women were hysterical, scores fainted; men wept as, in paroxysms of frenzy, they hurled themselves against the police lines.

In all, 146 people died in the Shirtwaist Factory fire: 123 women and girls, and 23 men. The oldest was 46, and the youngest 14 years old. Many were recent immigrants. Over 100,000 people joined in remembrance marches for them.

As for the two owners, they survived on the roof. They were acquitted of manslaughter charges, found guilty in a civil suit, but paid out a fraction per plaintiff of the overall insurance pay out. A couple of years later, one of the owners was found guilty of locking factory doors during working hours again. The judge was apologetic in fining him the minimum possible penalty of twenty dollars.

The Triangle Shirtwaist Factory fire remains one of the deadliest fires the United States has ever seen. It was to have a lasting impact.

Rights

The fire arrived at a time of an upswing in labor protests. A couple of years prior in 1909, the "Uprising of 20,000" had taken place in New York City, and walkouts and strikes had become common.

The fire was a galvanizing force on existing organizing. The International Ladies' Garment Workers' Union grew in size substantially in the aftermath. Focused largely on the work done by working-class women, which wasn't strongly represented in other textile unions with middle class memberships, they made themselves heard. In a speech after the fire labor leader Rose Schneiderman, a Polish immigrant, said:

> This is not the first time girls have been burned alive in the city. Every week I must learn of the untimely death of one of my sister workers. Every year thousands of us are maimed. The life of men and women is so cheap and property is so sacred. There are so many of us for one job it matters little if 146 of us are burned to death. We have *tried* you citizens; we are trying you now, and you have a couple of dollars for the sorrowing mothers, brothers and sisters by way of a charity gift. But every time the workers come out in the only way they know to protest against conditions which are unbearable the strong hand of the law is allowed to press down heavily upon us.

Public officials have only words of warning to us – warning that we must be intensely peaceable, and they have the workhouse just back of all their warnings. The strong hand of the law beats us back, when we rise, into the conditions that make life unbearable.

I can't talk fellowship to you who are gathered here. Too much blood has been spilled. I know from my experience it is up to the working people to save themselves. The only way they can save themselves is by a strong working-class movement.[2]

A change was in the air.

"My spirit revolts," said socialist and feminist Crystal Eastman, "when the dead bodies of girls are found piled up against locked doors after a factory fire, who wants to hear about a great relief fund? What we want is to start a revolution."[3]

Pushes again purchasing sweatshop-made items featured heavily on union-led posters of the time. Their concern was fair pay. With subsequent evolutions in labor law, sweatshops are now illegal in most western counties, but retail giants import cheaply produced clothes from developing countries. Modern labor reformers now take a more global interest in workers' rights and are joined in their protests by ecological campaigners, but some of the message has been caught up in brand-led marketing, selling the concept back to shoppers through a sense of virtuous, tasteful purchasing and lifestyle choices, communicated through seasonal trends.

Today, the fire is referenced by protestors and presidents, remembered as a catalyst for significant rights reforms including the Workers' Compensation Act, better sanitary and refreshment facilities for workers, and limits on working hours. There are still periodic memorials to the Triangle victims. For the centenary, a ceremony saw marchers hold aloft "shirtwaists" on poles, emblazoned with the names of the dead, while bells rang across the nation by individuals, firehouses, and schools.

Fire Safety

Modern fire signage regulations also owe a lot to the workers of the Shirtwaist Factory. Under union pressure, the Factory Investigating Commission was created by the New York State Legislature to investigate factory conditions and suggest legislation to prevent similar hazards and unsafe conditions. The Fire Department identified upwards of 200 factories vulnerable to similar catastrophe. In Britain, the Victoria Hall disaster in Sunderland in 1883 had also encouraged legal evolution on fire escape matters, following the deaths of 160 children; in similar circumstances, a door was bolted, preventing their escape.

Where once before legislation was scant, New York led the way for nationwide reform across the United States. New laws emerged on fire extinguishers, fireproofing procedures, egress, unobstructed exits, sprinklers, alarms, and lighted exit signs. The standardization of fire exit signs had begun.

4b THE POETICS OF EXIT DESIGN

Purpose

Exit signs are used every day, but it's for emergencies that they're ultimately designed. We need to know which way to go in one glance. Emergencies demand expedience and clarity; signs have evolved in response. An irony of some early exit signs is that they were intended to help people escape from the very circumstances likely to obscure the sign's visibility, clouded by smoke or extinguished by water. Our expectations to be protected and to be guided have evolved, too.

Much of the time to follow an exit sign is to walk through a door leading outside of a building or vehicle, or to be directed to a flight of stairs that will take us to such a door. In more complex scenarios, directional signs work in tandem not as individual, definitive-by-themselves signs, but as something akin to a trail of breadcrumbs. We might think we know where the exits of a plane are, when comfortably seated, but introduce darkness, confusion, and a bumpy ride and it becomes clear the dainty lights on the gangway aren't to bring a little ambiance to the red eye.

Perched above a door or in a corridor, the dark possibilities exit signs suggest are never far from us, but we have become accustomed to zoning out and ignoring them in our everyday, nonemergency lives. Enter the air steward to draw our attention to them in a series of choreographed, legally mandated, moves. We consider the likelihood of surviving by following the rules, obeying the directions of oxygen masks and life rafts, and go back to hoping we won't need them. In the worst emergency scenarios, the nightmare stuff of failure in the air or at sea, exit routes might be signaled, flashing, but unreachable: an instruction that cannot be carried out.

"The only thing airplane instruction cards really make clear is that the number of ways to express something in visual language may be even greater than in written language."[1]

In busy transport terminals, signs direct passengers to keep them from veering off and getting in harm's way. Museums use signs to funnel visitors to and through retail gauntlets. These kinds of signs are not "exit signs" per se, in terms of the legally recognized signs that are mandated for health and safety reasons, but we follow them expecting the same outcome, eventually, trusting in autopilot in their rationale.

I spoke to my friend Richard, an architect, about how it works from the planning side of things. He told me:

Arrows are always directing towards a "final exit," perhaps via a "storey exit," and the orientation of the arrows is important: arrows pointing diagonally down or up (to left or right) means a change of level is ahead in the direction indicated; an arrow pointing down means a change of level straight ahead; an arrow pointing upwards means straight ahead and may also indicate a change of level ahead; arrows to the left or right are just that, with no change of level.

In a retail arena, should there be a moral as well as safety imperative to provide clearly marked exit signs? To return visitors to spaces where they are no longer commercial targets, away from the multisensory noise and fuss of shopping? Should exit signs guide us out of scenarios which might harm our mental or financial as well as our physical health?

Design

A lot is expected of exit signs, placed in different scenarios of varying size and scale, with the same intended outcome. The design works hard and well.

After the Triangle Fire, with fire safety legislation developing rapidly, design guides became more specific. In the 1930s and 1940s, its focus was on the thickness of letters and overall legibility of the word EXIT. But a new problem arose: how to deliver crucial safety information to non-native speakers?

A couple of decades later, pictograms were taking off. First used as symbols to represent transport and toilet facilities, including on the London Underground, they eventually expanded to many different meanings. The picture-based code could be interpreted by speakers of varying languages, reducing confusion. In some cases, recognition of their meaning was faster than reading words.

"Icons are perceived as a whole, and this promotes fast processing. Language, by contrast, is read sequentially and therefore more slowly."[2]

The same communicative intention can be found in plastic food displays outside restaurants, most commonly in Japan (now more likely to be plastic than hand-painted), and photographs on menus, sending the additional signal of enticement to the hungry by constructing a 3D likeness of what they might eat.

When first introduced at the Olympics in 1964, pictograms felt modern and cool and received a subsequent boost in popularity, but they really fulfilled familiar functions not unlike prehistoric cave paintings and Egyptian hieroglyphs, or pictorial symbols in other early linguistic cultures. The word pictogram itself was a portmanteau of pictograph, meaning an image which represents something it resembles, and ideogram, a symbol representing an idea.

"The domain of icons exists at the border between language and perception, between abstract concepts and concrete objects."[3]

Sense of expectation is also crucial in imparting that meaning. Different actions might feasibly be taken in different places; if a sign was to be placed in an unusual or odd location, it might take longer to decipher its meaning. In some locations, we might anticipate risk, and a symbol such as an exit sign is confirmation of latent expectations of evacuation: To place the inverse of this idea in a ridiculous context, a symbol denoting washing instructions would likely cause significant confusion were it to be attached to an irrelevant object, such as a lightbulb. Fire exit symbols work because the concept of exit and evacuation is present across cultures, and the action they impart is compatible with cumulative associations.

Other than widespread use on health and safety and transport signs, the most common contemporary pictorial language system is emojis, which grew from the text-based smileys of the early internet into individual characters with increasingly advanced design. Although the symbols represent objects and moods, often they're used to creatively modify or supplement words, to add or intensify meaning. Sadly, there is no emoji for exit sign—yet.

Although standardization had been advanced legislatively across individual countries, calls to adopt a global exit sign, which could be understood by people of many languages, stepped up in the 1970s. A competition was held by a Japanese fire safety organization, with entrants from around the world. The winning design was by Yukio Oto: it is his running man on the cover of this book.

Curiously, his design shared eerie similarities with some other entrants, particularly from the Soviet Union. It was an indication that the basic design element, of a figure making its way through a doorway, was an intuitive depiction for the action of *exit* across cultures. With only minor details between them, Oto's design won out for its clarity.

Neither a pictogram of a running human, or the word exit itself, are made up of very many parts or shapes but boldly rendered in their most basic recognizable form. There's something elemental about these exit-humans that isn't a million miles away from early human forms in cave paintings, reduced to their most stark shapes, with no unnecessary flourishes to complicate our interpretation.

As a response to the need to stand out, exit signs are rendered in non-neutral, bold colors, typically red or green highly contrasted with white. If you look at an exit sign for sixty seconds and close your eyes, you are likely to still see it glowing on the inside of your eyelids.

Oto had been interested in pictograms for a while. In the mid 1970s he had developed the pictorial language LoCos; composed of a limited number of simple shape-based symbols such as modified triangles and lines, users could create sentences or meaning by arranging them in different combinations. The goal was to communicate universally without verbal language. His aim was to emphasize the importance of communication among all people of all the countries of the world.

It didn't really take off. But his goal was met with the design of the exit sign, which became used globally.

Exit signs are ordinarily utilitarian visual scaffolding. What's it like to put them in place? Richard: "I've never had a client who didn't want signs or had problems with where I'd sited them. Clients might not be keen to have 'panic hardware' on some doors—like a push bar to open—for aesthetic or security perspective. Similarly, with closers to doors—fire doors on escape routes have to be on automatic closers, to maintain compartmentation and preserve protected zones/routes/stairs—some people think they're inconvenient or annoying or something and remove them or use an object to prop them open (perhaps a handy fire extinguisher). This is bad."

In general usage, signs may be innocuous in their visual presence as I have described, but there are some examples of resentment, such as among some theater goers. Supposedly, they interrupt the *exits pursued by a bear* onstage by glowing persistently in the corners, and are a reminder of reality, unwanted and unwelcome, for the viewer who desires to totally suspend disbelief. Has our expectation of entertainment on demand, in the cocoon of our own homes, led to a break between plays and their environments, with demands for the theater's total atmospheric erasure? Or is it a harking back to tradition? There were no bright green signs in Shakespeare's day.

When a character exits the stage, as per direction, is the exit a one-time thing or is it a continuous action while she waits in the wings for her cue to return? The actor is not switched off, although his face and body may relax out of view of the audience. He may drink water that is not in the script. She stops performing, but does not relax. Does the character continue to exist while he's off the stage? I suppose he must, considered by the audience to be elsewhere. What if a character temporarily exits, and the actor takes suddenly ill and dies, never to return for later concluding scenes? Then the audience would need to exit for him.

Perhaps there is a latent desire for submission, in the desire for uninterrupted entrapment in pitch dark, entirely at the mercy of the players on stage without the green reminder we can leave anytime. Or perhaps audiences in the presence of acting have an impulse to insist upon their own free will and the exit sign is a little too much like a stage direction. The signs are here to stay, anyway. Audiences will continue holding contrasting versions of reality in their minds.

But when we need them, signs must be eye catching enough to be identified across a room. An exit sign must work to guide us whether we are wandering leisurely, walking purposefully, or instinctively fleeing. A desire for expediency is present when the sign is functioning in an everyday capacity, and when ideally our movement around or in and out of buildings is seamless and efficient. In an emergency, the expediency is urgent and essential. While the former performs as good design (not only of signs but of the buildings they're housed in), it's the latter that has really shaped the standardization (and associated legislation) of the crisp, clear imagery we see on exit signs.

Although defining how and when it is necessary to display exit signs can come down to individual jurisdictions that also often provide architects with updated guidance on compliance, the design of exit sign symbols, like other hazard and safety signs, is among those specified by the International Organization for Standardization (ISO), linking 164 voluntary membership countries in technical terminology, symbology, standards, and other information that facilitates trade and synchronizes safety. Existing in varying forms prior to the Second World War, during which it was suspended, the group was reshaped with UN encouragement in 1946.

It is the ISO, and specifically a group of symbols called the ISO 7010, that defines other familiar symbols, too. Yellow triangles stand for warnings, and it is perhaps the most exciting category, full of radioactive material and explosives. Slippery! Hot! Sharp! Guard dogs! Pop culture has often parodied warning signs. Music magazines have warned of explosive content inside. Associated signs and symbols can be found on T-shirts, badges, stickers, posters, and other lifestyle detritus, ranging from a kind of utilitarian chic to a general statement of protest and friction. Perhaps it's a safe way to hint at danger, the exoticism of toxicity made mundane and saleable.

Universality

Sign standardization is not without criticism or push for further improvements. The long process launched by the

Triangle Shirtwaist Fire is ongoing. More recent signage reflects not only technological advances but also evolving social insight. This should always be the case:

> Codes and standards are living documents. Born of the efforts of men and women to make their environment safer, codes and standards grow into maturity based on fire experience and the observations and research of those responsible for them. The best codes and standards [...] never age, as they are continually updated with new information that allows them to adapt to an ever-changing world.[4]

It's as recently as 2014 that the Accessible Exit Sign Project was established in Australia. Their tagline is "Everyone Deserves A Way Out of a Building" and their aim is lobbying lawmakers, architects and designers to take into consideration inclusive, universal accessibility. As a result of this and other campaign action, wheelchairs can now be found on some exit signs. When reflecting on the purpose of the exit sign in the first instance, to guide people out of a building with haste in the instance of emergencies, it's remarkable those with additional access requirements weren't already top priority. While fire safety laws are frequently revised, existing exits in older buildings are not one size fits all, particularly where there are stairs involved. The Global Alliance on Accessible Technologies and Environments (with the fitting acronym GAATES) have criticized signs that do not already contain inclusive design as discriminatory, advocating instead for signage such as the "accessible means of egress icon," a symbol of a wheelchair, to be used in tandem with the classic "running man" symbol.[5] The Egress Group, part of the project and providing "accessible exit sign solutions," have two designs registered:

> The combined "Running Man" and "Accessible Means of Egress Icon" are working together to escape the building. They move in unison, display the same urgency and motion and appear to be travelling at the same speed. Their heads are forward, showing their haste. Arms are extended and motioning back and forth as they move through the doorway.[6]

The International Organization for Standardization, which collected symbols under the grouping of ISO 7001 and which contains the original exit sign design, hasn't included an inclusive modified one. The Museum of Modern Art contains one among their collection. The Accessible Exit Sign Project continues.

Tech

Early signs pit available technology against environmental hazard and didn't fare especially well. A simple, nonelectronic sign painted with the word EXIT struggles to be seen in conditions of smoke or water, and when signs became electronically powered, they had the additional conundrum of withstanding power loss during outages likely in extreme weather conditions.

The immediacy that was demanded of the graphic design soon came to be understood in terms of disturbance to its use, with attempts to overcome the emergency conditions that were liable to get in the way of clear communication being built into the object design itself.

An early evolution was the reshaping of a two-dimensional sign into a box, so the word EXIT could be shown on both sides, illuminated by incandescent bulbs. Gradually, the problem of power going out and rendering the signs unlit was solved by connecting the power supply to backups, whether generator or battery powered—and was more successful still when batteries became smaller and more versatile than those of bulky size and limited charge. This allowed batteries to be fitted within the signs and do their work of powering illumination for longer. These evolving dual-power systems solved some problems, but there were still many changes to be made to improve the general efficiency of the signs.

After outages, another major problem was penetrating smoky or dim conditions with a light bright enough to be seen, especially important in the case of fire. Early emergency signage was easily obscured until incandescent bulbs gave way to something brighter; fluorescents and light-emitting diodes allowed for a much stronger light, with the additional benefit of requiring less power, and signs became more dependable in disasters.

Exit signs are permanent fixtures and might be required at any time of day: Disasters don't bed down for the night. This means signs must constantly be switched on. The long life of LEDs means they have to be changed much less frequently than a bulb; this also absorbs some of the upkeep pitfalls of human error or oversight.

The vast majority of illuminated exit signs operate in these ways, although phosphorescent and radioluminescent signs have also existed since the 1970s, using, respectively, glow-in-the-dark phosphors or the radioactive properties of tritium gas as sources of illumination.

In Situ

The exit sign is, ultimately, only one part of a wider legal and physical system ordered in particular ways to keep humans safe. Just as the interpretation of the sign is a communicative pact between its design and human consciousness, so too are there responsibilities in the environment and circumstances of their placement.

Richard's still with us: "Architects have got to be methodical and look at things from each perspective to make sure it's compliant but also that a building will work for its users in all foreseeable circumstances."

The design of the sign itself, no matter how crisp and expedient in its delivery of information, would be meaningless if it were left in a cupboard, as would an arrow pointing in the wrong direction, away from a staircase to freedom. The responsibility of communication lies not only with the designer, but on the person ordering such signs and affixing them, within the context of an architect's placement of doors and passageways.

Would an exit sign really be an exit sign if it were pointing at a brick wall instead of a door? Is an exit sign an exit sign if it doesn't work?

Fire safety signs must be placed in relationship to universally accessible exit routes, as well as signaling evacuation devices and areas of refuge, all of which are the subject of ongoing developments in law, along with specifications pertaining to the width of passageways that can accommodate wheelchairs, and the doorway dimensions of buildings hosting large numbers of workers. But bureaucracy can get in the way of progress. What might have been approved by one organization is rejected by another; national and international guidance may differ.

Too often people are let down by the practical application of mobility devices. I once was stuck in an accessible glass elevator in an airport for around half an hour. Other than the panic attack, I felt angry and indignant not to have been immediately rescued. But had my life been different,

I might have been less surprised at the lack of answer to the call button. It can take a surprisingly long time for ramps and tunnels to be connected to planes, and the green light given to release passengers to disembark, with the buck for frequent wheelchair losses and damage being passed between airlines and airports. In 2010, budget UK airline easyJet was criticized for banning wheelchairs altogether, blaming weight restrictions and health and safety regulations, while fitting as many seats as possible on the plane to maximize ticket sales. Some budget airlines have also considered charging passengers to use the on-flight bathroom. Exiting a vehicle is as necessary to travelling somewhere as the engine of the plane itself; this basic functionality should be the same for any passenger with a ticket to ride.

4c THE FUTURE OF EXIT SIGNS

Some fire safety experts and policy researchers are proponents of adaptable exit signage, which would take the existing design and add elements that are moldable in some way: at its simplest, this is the addition of flashing lights; at its most complex, adaptive exit signs could change depending on the nature of the threat in order to give the most useful information, such as the difference between an active shooter and a fire. They might possibly give more nuanced information as to which direction is best, diverting away from exits compromised.

The problem is, we could do this very easily with current technology. It would be simple for us to hook up a sign, and to accompany it, cameras set up to monitor the area in order to inform what should go on the sign. But if this all were to happen, it would require constant human observation. How many businesses or schools would pay for someone to sit and watch, waiting possibly endlessly for something to occur to prompt them to change the sign? Some complex risk spaces like airports have constant monitoring, but are typically (these days, at least) at an enduringly heightened level of national security, with information gathering occurring in tandem with immediate safety concerns. Other places with closed-circuit TV (CCTV) may be mass monitored, in law enforcement centers with multiple screens on the wall. But the vast majority of CCTV cameras record on finite "tapes," resetting themselves or storing only temporarily, never to be watched by a human being. Even where they are required, by law enforcement or proprietors seeking information on a break-in, they can be unreliable, prone to failure, self-erasure, or be too low in quality to be useful. Not everything can be captured, just as not every exit is straightforward. Humans, perhaps, behave in less predictable ways than any other challenge to the ordering of physical spaces and our passage through them.

But if airports pose high enough risks that constant monitoring can occur, couldn't the same argument be made for schools with rising numbers of shootings? Aren't schools becoming critical places for security, with high risks? I am not arguing for policing in schools, which has led to incidents of racial violence, revealed by the constant monitoring potential of fellow students' phones. But the question is, where are citizens willing to invest in safety? Are ideas of where danger lurks still to catch up with school shootings, when it comes to government spending and resources?

There's also the suggestion that exit signs with flashing lights might be more effective than the current static incarnation, for example, in areas competing for visual attention such as airports and shopping centers, making them more attention grabbing. Many public spaces, whether retail or transport (with increasingly blurred lines between them), are heady places, with signage everywhere, promotional slogans screaming from shop windows in bright colors, moving parts in window displays, free samples, music, audio promotions, charity donation groups (known as "chuggers" in the UK, a portmanteau of "charity muggers"), food court aromas, packed crowds, entertainment pavilions, and the overall impetus to buy, buy, buy. All these elements are competing with essential signage for our attention. There is physical confusion at play, too, in commonplace illusions of free will; the supermarkets and shops which set out their floor plans in consultation with psychological studies and market research to encourage shoppers to follow the route most likely to purchase the most number of items, rather than the most efficient one.

In 2018, a story about IKEA directional guides went viral. The Swedish home furnishings store is known for its elaborate floor plans that take customers on a journey through different themed zones corresponding to areas of the home. First there are showroom examples, displaying rooms of houses done up in the latest products to spark inspiration in impulse-buying browsers, before they are directed through sectioned shopping bays selling first kitchen products, and then bathroom products, and later houseplants and large furniture items, all in one meandering line rather than the more frequent "bays" arrangement of other large shops, which take subtler approaches in their prompting, such as in placing commonly purchased items at their rear to increase time spent in store, or flagging bargain buys as enticements. We have come to view a trip to IKEA as an "experience" culminating in Swedish meatballs and loganberry soda, which is of course another spending opportunity as much as it has become a tradition or a treat for making it all the way round. Gripes are often not about the floor plan design, but about how busy it can be on holidays. The system is generally accepted, considered part and parcel of the IKEA brand, aided by their commitment to it over many years. A fake news article claimed a man was arrested for placing fake arrows on the floor of IKEA to send customers in circles; perhaps we were so willing to collectively take the story at face value because it taps into a latent fear of never-ending shopping trips where we feel weary, overstimulated, and gradually lose control of our willpower, at the mercy of the shops themselves to guide us onwards, carried by their momentum before resurfacing at the other end with more shopping bags than anticipated. Although the pathways, so clearly laid out, highly discourage customers from wandering off, there is nothing to stop us finding shortcuts by squeezing through displays, but we rarely do.

Some airport departure lounges have lined walkways with retail opportunities, which passengers must traverse to get to their necessary location. I have walked an unnecessarily long passage in a London airport several times and each time felt robbed of some perceived but intangible right to get where I needed to be by the most expedient and hassle-free route. Captive audiences spend; retail is a form of entertainment. But the emphasis on schedules and arriving at the gate on time makes being subjected to retail bombardment a condition of passage, an uneasy match, and an anxiety-increasing prospect.

This problem of competing atmospheric noise, and any evolution of the current signage to tackle it, is really a return to concerns raised from its earliest development, where lighting was added to make signs stand out more. This isn't necessarily a *flaw* in the sign, but even the exit sign's already modified version has diminished within the ever-evolving environment surrounding it. Our worlds continue to grow more visually complex and demanding, with an increasing percentage of everyday life requirements across work, personal admin, and entertainment, conducted in online spaces with the potential to distract in a different dimensional way. In such a saturated landscape, our physical and mental exits might not always be in sync.

To be static, like current exit sign designs, has now become unfit to compete for attention. To be static is incompatible with the rapidity and rush of modern life, which is also reflected in how we communicate, increasingly with bombast rather than stillness or nuance. Reaction videos, which show people's faces as they watch videos or listen to music, have flooded YouTube, overexaggerated expressions gripping human faces like rigor mortis is beginning to set in. (2020

ACADEMY AWARD REACTIONS! CATS REACTION TO CAT FILTER! GROWN MAN CRIES WHEN WWE WRESTLER RETURNS!) They're hugely popular, but if one draw is to feel companionship in our own feelings about a piece of pop culture, the loud performativity of them seems to get in the way of an intimate connection; it's more like a sideshow mirror where a distorted, extreme version of ourselves leaps out. Our interactions can be brash and blunt to bridge gaps, or to take advantage for malevolent impulses. Complex subjects are reduced to headlines and clickbait and experts are derided. (Most nakedly, when the British cabinet's Michael Gove claimed in 2016 that "people are tired of experts," when the infeasibility of Brexit became clear from expert and industry reports.) I'm conscious that this is a generalization, but it is reflective of trend. Our politics, now barely distinguishable from entertainment, has become more polarized, news and current affair programming has fallen victim to "both sides" editorial fallacies, which reduces nuanced topics to "sides" in staged debates, often using human rights as fodder, then uploaded online by networks themselves as inflammatory clips. (PIERS MORGAN'S PASSIONATE GENDER RANT!) We fall into "silos"[1] of news opinions, consuming more and more what we already agree with, as it appears tailored for us on timelines; the polarizing politicians play to this gallery, a significant step more concerning than speaking in sound bites for media pickup. The texture of public communication is increasingly startling, as if everything is rendered in bold, and just like the design of essential signs, intended to be communicated in an instant, signaling wider political and social contexts, some extremist and disturbing.

But I digress. Critics of overreliance on mobile phones and internet usage often complain of a "bubble." To me, it feels instead like the visual information atmosphere we exist within is more of an electronic sprawl, extending into the distance and as far as the eye can see. I agree we can get lost in it. A flashier sign combats the environment around us mentally just as much as physically. The problem is not our ability to see it, as once we look we can see it clearly, as it was designed. The problem is that it takes us a while to focus on it in a sea of all the other information diverting our eyes and attention, and perhaps skewing our sense of security and danger, too.

Sign design, like the safety codes, must always be updated. Design responds to atmosphere. Then there is a more complex environment, followed by more sophisticated design, until the environment becomes even more complex and overwhelms the sign once again, and the pattern repeats; the most recent phase of this cycle is complex visual and sensory environments rather than smoke and power outages. In the UK, we do not have amber alerts which appear on phones, but their ability to break through very decisively seems elemental, immediately demanding focus in a cramped and compulsive information arena. Signs will change like modern environments change, tumbling after one another into the distance, for infinity.

Overcoming distraction is an old problem in a new scenario. In the end, decisions must be rubber stamped by official health and safety codes, balancing—as well as environmental changes—technological advances and individual rights and applying new information. The only thing that isn't coming around again is standardization; that's a sort of one-time deal. Technology development and the evolution of safety laws in response to demands for rights have been the biggest drivers of changes to exit signs to date. The biggest driver for safety signage modification in the future looks likely to be universal engagement with accessibility (although this is also about technology and rights).

Innovation in information signaling (outside of safety codes) is otherwise driven by everything from propaganda to commercialism. Recently, it has been possible to make animated signs in the night sky using drones with lights. In videos from such a display in China, onlookers gasp and react to the image of a walking human figure stepping off a high-rise tower into the dark sky, moving its limbs in midair. An animated computer-generated imagery (CGI) sequence in the form of a golden lion prowled the Estudiantes stadium in Argentina before a football game. These are grand and spectacular illusions, but also a little frightening in their implications for where information might be placed in future. Some high-rise buildings have been entirely plastered in programmable LEDs, resulting in moving images spanning one or even a series of tower blocks and other buildings around cities. The graphic texture of the world is changing around us at a faster pace than previous evolutions of signmaking and communicative technology, from papyrus to the printing press and the internet's arrival. A pessimist would say that there is now no space left that isn't vulnerable to commercial (or propaganda) modification through its surface area being transformed. It is hard to disagree. We are also in an era where organic land is in swift decline. The surface area of livable land is eroding from climate change–related pressures. Coral reefs and forests are being destroyed at an exponential rate. Taken separately, these factors feel distant from the lives of ordinary working people in areas that on the surface seem relatively unaffected. But a pattern is emergent. A different kind of exit.

If exit signs were modifiable, they would also be hackable. The artist Jenny Holzer[2] "hacks" the idea of signs by placing her own, frequently with anti-consumerist, anti-capitalist messaging, in public spaces, and utilizes ticker-tape-style banners to broadcast countercultural messages, such as her giant mounted electronic signs looming over busy city streets that read "ABUSE OF POWER COMES AS NO SURPRISE" and "PROTECT ME FROM WHAT I WANT." Some slogans were reused in her work *Blue Purple Tilt*, a row of ticker-tape-style signs propped against a wall in soothing, feminine shades of purple and blue. Her choice of objects and language merges the utilitarian with the fantasy, taking hard aim at violence in society, with targets including gun lobbyists and the military-industrial complex.

We are used to signs directing us to follow instructions and keep things moving.; often they keep the peace, preventing accidents and guiding movement through cities. But Holzer's signs are subversive, situating criticism within symbols of ordinary, everyday life. Our willingness to follow directions is disrupted, and so are graphic displays in the public realm: billboards, neon, plaques, and carvings.

These communication spaces are difficult to "unlock" and repurpose, but Holzer has done so, outside of a gallery setting in prominent locations such as in front of Trump Tower.[3] By putting her message on wheels, the artist gets it into the public realm of signage, utilizing the means of traffic signage and advertising (which are frequent) but hijacking it for political protest (which is not). The blocky titling of Trump Tower, clad in garish gold, is inverted in the stark signs. Signs typically belong to cities and governments, not people. But what if they gave us different directions? Holzer's signs are a reclamation of public space in public interest.

Were exit signs digitally modifiable, crucial components of public safety could also be amended by bad actors, exploited in terrorist or shooting incidents, or subject to the errors of digital malfunctioning or spamming spyware. The occasional screen in public life falls victim to digital error; this can occasionally be seen on travel screens, bank machines, and anywhere else utilizing screens, where the promised information has exited the stage, often replaced by error codes or digital glitching. But even this problem isn't new. This is a kind of repeat of early bulbs failing, succumbing to design flaws. Backups and safeguarding measures are then inevitably invented, just as generator power access was enabled for lighted signs decades ago. These are not the only scenarios. Bored teenagers are the bane of every mall. Imagine the possibilities, ranging from malicious to benign, if they hacked the building itself, taking over its signage. One of my favorite instances of a harmless error on Twitter, not a hack but seemingly a mix-up of user accounts, was when a young worker went live on camera with a "wine cuz bored" caption from the official Glasgow City Council account, which typically tweets traffic, event, and other functional or bureaucratic information for locals.

While searching for exit sign videos on YouTube, I found an exit-themed playlist[4] that was mostly clips of teenagers smashing exit signs in their schools with baseball bats and other weapons—the kind of mindless, petty destruction that blights schools everywhere. The titles include the simple, depersonalized "Exit Sign Smash" and "Exit Sign Kicking," and the claim "He Hates Exit Signs." According to other videos on the playlist, Leandro hates all exit signs and Tyler attacks one. In one very grainy, large pixel clip from 2008 titled "Head Hits Exit Sign," the exit sign fights back, and a young man runs away clutching his head with an "ow" after jumping and heading it. "Mouse in an exit sign" is a gremlin in the machine. A couple are explicitly interested in functionality, recording "new" signs, sign performance during specific emergency scenarios, or signs with a particular lighting setup. But most of these videos are, in some way, negatively (if not outright violently) framed. The sign is personified with "Poor Exit Sign Dies." It is not, as one might assume, a video of a sign failing to light up, but a person standing at the top of a cement staircase holding an exit sign in one hand, which they then proceed to drop. It smashes into hundreds of pieces, white against the grey ground. The video is forty seconds long, but the action is over in no more than two. It ends with a close-up of the carnage.

Who compiled it, and took an interest in the intersection of mindless violence and our built environments? I can't ascribe motive to a low-info YouTube account, but in looking at their curated collection of destruction and malfunctions wondered to what extent our interests overlapped. This led me to the realization that although I didn't demonstrate it by destroying those around me, my own lure was the surreal and subversive potential of the signs—in other words, a flipping upside down of the reality around me. We had in common a desire for an altered reality, whether latently hostile to the signs or drawn toward the possibilities of what else might take their place.

5 GROUCHLAND: BREXIT, SESAME STREET, AND GARBAGE

Brexit

Brexit was always a hole through which meaning could fall.

As I write this book, the exit is looming. As I sat in a lounge overlooking London Euston train station concourse, a giant electronic sign above the heads of passengers played *Get Ready for Brexit* advertisements on a loop, side by side with cancellations and delays on the departure board. The Overton window of Brexit's surreality danced around like an old Windows screensaver whose cursor doesn't work.

The clock has been ticking down to final exit for over a year, and with shambolic negotiations between the UK and the European Union (EU) ongoing and the country's citizens fiercely split on the matter, no one knows what will happen next, other than that it will either be very bad, or very, very bad. Brexit was an exit with no entrance in sight; no plans, no strategy. It was exit into fantasyland—undefined but glorious. For some, with little hope in incremental political change, having been let down by it before, that sounded better than what they saw around them.

From its offing, Brexit was a project characterized by absence of details, misinformation, and vagary. It was a mirage, far off and promising what was not really there, most memorably in the disproven Leave campaign claim, emblazoned on the side of a red bus, that an additional £350 million per week might be re-routed into the National Health Service (NHS).[1] It will not, for it does not exist.

Scotland still has an escape route; the campaign for its independence from the UK is ongoing. Now, it would be an exit from an exit. Unlike the Brexit campaign, the Scottish independence debate in 2014 was information heavy. Citizens were provided with a white paper for a plan that they might choose to advance or reject, and it was heartily scrutinized. In the months leading up to the vote on September 19 of that year, it was almost impossible to walk into a pub or stand at a bus stop without overhearing conversations about it, sometimes between strangers, and often detailed enough to stray into the waters of fishing law or currency options. The result went narrowly to No, but after the process, it felt, overall, that the general populace had engaged in healthy and violence-free debate, in the meantime learning anew about their country, how it works, and considering what they might want for its future. The distance between Scottish views on Brexit and the UK's as a whole has refueled and increased interest for Scottish independence. Yes badges, symbols of the independence campaign when the option on the ballot paper was yes for independence, have been re-appearing on lapels in a new design,[2] their bars of color speaking of plurality and modularity.

In contrast, the question of Brexit was horoscope-like in its shapeless form, an empty box with citizens prompted to fill it with their projected hopes and fears; meanings expanding to fill the available space, of which there was plenty. Bad actors traded on racist, xenophobic, populist tub-thumping and aims to profit from the carnage (most concerningly, with an eye on the NHS). Weaknesses in the system were exposed. Digital spending skirted electoral rules, the working knowledge Brits had of the existing EU relationship was shown to be appallingly scant. Brexit jammed a crowbar into the already present cracks in traditional media. Disinformation ran rampant—as it was doing everywhere else in the world.

Other than the individual motives of its agitators, the project stood for nothing at all, and was granted a name accordingly. Brexit, for *British Exit*. The name was originally laughed at for its crunchy breakfast cereal sound. But it caught on. Politicians of all parties tried to add meaning to it with adjectives, but this made it even more confusing and abstracted; you cannot modify the meaning of nothing.

"I'm interested in all these terms that have been identified—hard Brexit, soft Brexit, black Brexit, white Brexit, grey Brexit—

and actually what we should be looking for is a red, white and blue Brexit,"[3] said then Prime Minister Theresa May, missing out on green Brexit, which had also been proposed. The Dutch Foreign Minister went to greater effort in conceptualizing Brexit with a giant, blue, fuzzy mascot wearing a T-shirt reading "Brexit," depicted as getting in everyone's way;[4] foreign media rightfully mocked the lack of strategy.

Each time a new menu option emerged, it was soon followed by its opposite, representing the divide but little else. Hard, soft, black, white, spinning as if by centrifugal force. What was at stake, requiring hundreds of civil servants to examine thousands of laws, industry projections spreading the breadth and width of the country, and other constitutional matters hanging in the balance, was reduced to nonsense words, devoid of detail, meaning, or sense. It was chaos politically and linguistically. Writing on violence and inequality, Rebecca Solnit has said:

> Calling things by their true names can also cut through the lies that excuse, disguise, avoid or encourage inaction, indifference, and obliviousness in the face of injustice and violence.[5]

Brexit has demonstrated the political risk of imprecise language, in a world where the meaning of truth is being degraded by presidents, broadcast media fallacy of balance has been exploited by alt-right conspiracists, and experts have been derided as "elite."

Hannah Arendt once wrote, "the ideal subject of totalitarian rule is [...] people for whom the distinction between fact and fiction (i.e. the reality of experience) and the distinction between true and false (i.e. the standards of thought) no longer exist."[6]

May tried to put the subject to rest with "Brexit means Brexit,"[7] a tautology in which the nullity cannibalizes itself. In one way, the nonsensical language fit the nonsensical politics behind Brexit. But in its imprecision, pro Brexit slogans fueled live time myth making about the country. Ideas of taking back control merged with turning back the clock. The most ardent, not only on the Leave side, spoke with pride and nostalgia for a version of Britain that never existed, while wars were evoked by those who never experienced them, justifying hostility to "foreigners" and decrying younger generations who had voted differently.

No matter what the constitutional and trade situation is by the point you are reading these lines, the entrance that always follows an exit was in Brexit's case a one-way ticket to the realm of absurdity, a degradation of our democracy at the cost of truth.

Sesame Street

Sesame Street has a surprising number of songs about Exits.

In 1974, *Sesame Street* ran a song written by Chris Cerf and Norman Stiles called "Exit," about feeling stuck in life.

"Just get right up, and walk right out, that good old exit."[8] The piano player and two back-up singers perform under an Exit sign and audience members take their advice until the room is empty, the singer's voice echoing. The piece closes with his cry of help, as he is unable to find the exit himself. (Maybe I've found the source of that dream after all . . .)

There is a collaboration with Keith Haring set to a hip-hop beat, where kids dancing to an illustrated backdrop leave through the EXIT when the bell rings. Haring's figures pop off the wall and exit, too.[9]

Grover explains exit and spells the word out. "When you are inside someplace, and you are looking for a way to get out, what you do is, you look at an exit sign, and the exit sign really says Hey guys, this is the way out!" Standing in front of the sign, he is trampled by those on their way out. He adds "An exit can also be an entrance!" and is trampled again as the hordes come back through the door.[10]

"Everyone out of the exit door,"[11] goes a song accompanying a guide to the letter X, shown in situ in EXIT, as a parade of animals filters through, slamming the door behind them. Elsewhere, E is for Enter and Exit, and while the narrator is trying to explain this, a character in the background goes in one door and out the other repeatedly. In another clip, a man faced on all directions by brick walls pushes at them to no avail, until an Exit sign drops out of the sky, and when he affixes it to one wall, it swings open. SuperGrover (obviously, a different character from Grover, despite their similarities),

72 **EXIT**

gets stuck between the metal bars of a park trying to can rescue a stuck boy, who ends up finding the Exit sign and wandering off. A Charlie Chaplin look-alike falls prey to a sneakily moving exit sign, opening doors repeatedly to find brick walls behind them. A husky-voiced bear wearing a fedora carries a big red exit sign through a colorful landscape to the soundtrack of jazz. To the beat of drums, a squeaky orange ball rolls through a dark blue labyrinth following exit signs, reading the word aloud at each pass. A figure travels shuttles between exit signs pointing at one another, growing more and more frustrated until he just breaks a hole in the wall.

Although they jump around and cause mischief, EXIT signs in *Sesame Street* always result in one thing: animals, people, and objects follow the arrows with eventual success. This gleeful, musical, psychedelic nonsense has more internal logic than Brexit.

Sesame Street has a classic outsider figure in Oscar the Grouch, who says he's down on the idea of love, but also sings a song called "I Love Trash"[12] in which he cradles a worn old sneaker given to him by his mother the day he was born. Although he distances himself emotionally, he has an ability to see value in things others do not. I feel kinship with him in his joy in the mundane. Perhaps anyone reading an Object Lessons book will get it. Some of the most interesting scenes with Oscar take place in Grouchland, the alternative realm inside his trash can, a sort of internal exit from Sesame Street. The Grouch demonstrates that the trash can is deceptive in size, as is perception from the outside, when he engages with other characters by producing a surprising array of objects.

The expansive trash universe is a deeper and richer existence than onlookers might credit the Grouch with: All that can be seen of it from Sesame Street is its exterior, a battered old can. The moral is of understanding and not judging by appearances, and it's taken in the suitably comic direction of the mismatched spatial dimensions at either side of the portal. The Grouch shares similarities with grumpy orange feline Garfield—it has been speculated that Garfield doesn't really hate Mondays, but rather dislikes his owner Jon leaving for work.[13]

What Oscar has that most other residents of Sesame Street do not is the ability to exit everyday normal reality and enter a realm in which he is in his element, at ease, and ennobled with power. Besides, he has a cool worm friend in Slimey, a creature similarly on the margins of the *Sesame Street* society, and Oscar looks out for him by teaching his little friend to cross a tiny street. "Why not? They have places to go!"[14] When an onlooker challenges Oscar and says the setup is not a real street, Oscar proves him wrong by telling another worm friend sitting in the model car that he can go home now, and it drives off. Slimey and Oscar hang out together in the mutual understanding of their class, a little to the edge of a universe that is generally kind and benevolent. By the logic of the *Sesame Street* universe, even life on the margins is peachy. It might be trash, but it's their trash.

As Helen Adam, the poet who had to exit one place to be able to fully realize herself in another wrote,

> Let that prophet of beauty
> Live with ugliness.
> The wise may see
> From the city dump
> The world of Blake,
> The Blazing sunflower.[15]

Garbage

In the last few years, a subculture celebrating trash-adjacent, anti-social animals has emerged online. The zeitgeist captured best by a Twitter account, @binanimals,[16] which shares images of scavenging creatures such as raccoons, pigeons, and the ibis (known in Australia and New Zealand as a "bin chicken"). Captions are often explicitly political, always rooting for the working classes, and with an anarchist or Robin Hood flavor. As squirrels run away with stolen goods, the wider context is how animals respond and adapt to the detritus of our messy, urban lifestyles and Capitalism's excessive detritus and garbage, and how they meet their needs to live and eat in the same spaces. It makes explicit how garbage doesn't just disappear when it exits our apartments and factories.

Other malevolent animals have captured attention in recent years, particularly mean avians like the horrible goose in Untitled Goose Game (HONK!) and a cassowary that murdered its owner and subsequently went viral as a "giant murder bird."[17] Followers cheer on clips of subway rats dragging slices of pizza bigger than their own bodies with a whisper of latent desire to see nature take over and upend our daily lives, to overturn their low ranking in the pecking order by finding pleasure where they can. Raccoons breaking into bins and seagulls stealing chips express some of the same needs and impulses we have, in a more explicit, carnally base way, and celebrating them is a way for millennials and Gen Y/Zers to let off steam, facing the epic political environmental tragedies unfolding daily and in a more financially precarious position than their predecessor generations. There is a subtle pessimistic undertone in these celebrations of anarchy and pleasure: an acknowledgement that the daily working grind is difficult to escape from, and that there are few exits. That the wins, though sweet, are small, sensual, and temporary.

I notice garbage most when I'm walking around a city alone, especially a city bigger than I'm used to, which is when I'm at my most observant, a little amped up on adventure, a little cautious. I twist my head to look down alleyways. I wonder what's behind doorways. I look at the ground. Something moves me and I stop to take a photograph of it, trying to capture what I can't put into words, usually a sense of intimacy, from a distance. Garbage is the ruins of everyday living, thrown out with stories contained in it. Garbage can be beautiful. Kale leaves make for excellent garbage, strewn on top of a bin or on the ground near a market stall. Long, curving, dark green leaves with their flamboyant curlicues, bending their backs like dancers. Glass bottles lined up waiting to ring out five different notes. Unexpected colors of plastic bags among the black and greys: bubblegum pink, pool blue. Logos on local pizza boxes are someone's pride, someone's name. But where does it go?

"Disorient" by Fiona Tan[18] is a video installation that uses two facing screens to juxtapose soft shots of pretty Far East trinkets on the shelves of a quiet store with scenes of pollution, gigantic waste dumps, and worker exploitation, linking what citizens of the west might buy on a whim with their conditions of existence in other countries. Viewers must turn their back to one screen to watch the other, showing an inability to put the two together simultaneously.

There are cases of reversal of dumping in some Southeast Asian countries returning waste to the west, in the form of plastic and electronic waste, and sometimes falsely declared imports. The gravity of the repercussions deepened a few years ago when China halted their processing of metal and plastic waste, resulting in other countries in the region facing an increase in discarded toxic waste coming their way. In the run-up to 2020's Basel Convention, which deals with the global disposal of toxic waste, political opposition is becoming stronger. "Malaysia will not be the dumping ground of the West,"[19] said Environmental Minister Yeo Bee Yin, taking a stand during a photo call beside rubbish-packed containers filled with milk cartons and CDs, soon to return to their country of origin. Indonesia and the Philippines have also returned crates to their original European, Australian, and American origins, physically sending the stuff back to be dealt with at source. The economic injustice of wealthy countries sending their waste elsewhere is even grosser than the stuff itself. Some men are reported to avoid environmentally friendly behavior because they fear it may come across as "gay."[20] As Twitter user @no1guncle tweeted, "New research shows toxic masculinity to be toxic."[21] For many in wealthy nations, even where there are local issues with refuse disposal, we drop litter, and it falls into the black hole of our consciousness. We assume the city takes care of it for us, and don't think much about where it goes next.

In Spain in the summer of 2019, a judge ruled that a man who had videoed himself throwing a fridge over a steep cliff while joking about recycling must retrieve and dispose of it in the correct manner.[22] There is something biblical, and very satisfying in a way that is not entirely kind, in seeing him tussle in the dirt with his burden, the ghost of white goods come back from its afterlife to haunt him.

In the spring of 2019, in protest against the environmental impact of energy and waste, campaign group Greenpeace erected the words LAST EXIT sculpted from giant blocks of ice in front of Berlin's Brandenburg Gate. It was a reminder that our current system cannot hold forever; that those in positions of relative comfort, not faced with the waste of the western world, will be caught up with it eventually as the world warps further.

Exits and entrances are always two sides of the same coin. We spin it so that it blurs and becomes indistinct, but heads or tails, it's always going to fall flat, some time.

6 ELEVATION

The short film *Lift* begins with an elevator car shot from above, squeaking methodically down the long cables of its shaft while an overlay of resident voices can be heard distantly, hinting at the lives beyond the mechanism. A second shot is the tower block from outside, stretching up at least fifteen stories or more, silhouetted against a dark snow-filled sky. A smattering of lights in the uniformly square windows look yellow and warm. We next see the elevator empty but for the reflection of Mark Isaacs with his camera in the fuzzy ceiling mirror. When residents begin to appear, most of them are dressed for protection against the chill. The color palette is mostly muted grey, green, and navy, colors of Britain in wintertime, until an elderly woman in a purple coat fills the frame, which is limited to the inside of the small lift and pointed at the doorway. She giggles conspiratorially with the filmmaker, having taken it upon herself to establish a sense of order. "You can't come in yet, they're filming, he's a reporter," she bossily instructs another resident. As the camera zooms in, the lines of mirth on her powdered face are replaced with a sense of curiosity verging on doubt. "Well, we're here. Mazel Tov," she says on departing at her floor, with cheer returning to her face.[1]

To make the 25-minute film, Isaacs set himself up inside the London high rise for ten hours a day over two months, filming residents going in and out and reacting and interacting with his camera. The small, perfunctory space is immediately transformed into an intriguing performance stage.

In Britain, "flats" emerged midcentury as a public housing strategy to accommodate high volumes of residents in sanitary and safe conditions, replacing slums and war-damaged areas. Residents, typically working class, pay rent to the local council. In the run-up to this period, architectural influences included Le Corbusier, and some feted and now very expensive, privately owned Brutalist buildings like the Barbican estate in London emerged in a similar time period. Although there is an urban blockiness in their construction, most tower blocks in comparison were not intricately designed, nor built to last as long, appearing like tall thin cuboids on the horizon. Some older long-term residents speak highly of a community feel present in the early days, when such developments were at the peak of their desirability, but as the "streets in the sky" dream gave way, there was a pervading sense of isolation. The older woman in the purple coat is filmed lamenting how much the local area has changed since her friends in the building have moved away. "It was paradise. Now I've got double upstairs, drilling and banging . . ." We are let into her life, just a little. Despite intentions of wider development of the less populous (and less expensive) land planners favored for their construction, the buildings can suffer from poor integration into surrounding areas and estates (a counterpart to American "projects"), compounded by their frequent situation in areas with higher factors of low employment, poor transport links, and overall lack of investment.

Living vertically, many floors of residents atop the other, leaves few spaces to congregate socially and the buildings typically have little or no communal space outside, leaving bored teenagers to loiter on the periphery like seagulls. Inhabitants bump into one another as they are coming or going, such as in the elevator. One of the factors which made Isaacs's film so suspenseful is that in tower block lifts, passengers never know who will be there when the doors open, and this is successfully replicated from the viewer's perspective. In this way, residents are taken by surprise by the camera. Gradually they grow used to it, and some begin to interact with it. One man often appears on his way to or from the pub, confiding his lack of success in finding a date, as though the small space were a confessional. Later in the film, he tells the camera that he quit his job, and seems to be looking forward to a new beginning. Others ignore the camera, and in these situations the tension is palpable. There is a touching moment when a man brings Isaacs some food, showing hospitality for this stranger on the threshold of his home, bringing it out of his plastic bag to share. A different man who appears several times with a composed but taciturn manner eventually reveals he recently suffered the personal loss of more than one family member. His scenes are haunting, both the restrained delivery, which retrospectively reads as shock, and the sudden vulnerability. The last we see of him is stepping out of the doors. In the aftermath of the film, it was reported that this man died by suicide.

There's something comforting in the film's depiction of daily mundanity, as the camera slowly draws out its humane possibilities. This space represents moments of the passengers' lives that are neither here nor there. Everyone who steps into the lift is on their way in or out. Everyone has crossed a threshold of one exit, or another.

There's something disorienting about the overhead lighting, bouncing off the steel of the boxy elevator no matter what time of day it might be outdoors, and residents enliven the space with their presence. It's an unexpected venue for *something happening*; all the more surprising to see the self-reflection of strangers through the camera lens, confronted with their own curiosity, and opening up to it. They perform, drawing out elements of their personalities or aspects of their lives from under the surface, things they ordinarily wouldn't reveal while in the stage of exiting (or entering) their homes; we see this in admissions of bereavement, dissatisfaction, and loneliness as much as in conviviality and friendship.

Although it can be depressing, I feel soothed by the film, in tune with its emotional frequency. Perhaps it's watching people turn what is a rather lonely space, not designed for either lingering nor impactful interactions, into a space of meaning, and imparting a sense of ownership over a space that is uncertain by being neither one thing nor the other—it's not home, it's not outdoors, it's never the destination in itself. But here the lift becomes the central space, rather than an in-between one. It's not quite community, but it is a one-to-one interaction: the passengers coming face to face with themselves, rather than zoning out on their way in or out the building.

Highs and Lows

I once had a publishing job that was, on paper, a good one, but where each day became a repeat of the one before, not helped by the literal and metaphorical gloom of a walk down a long dusty road to a bleak industrial estate, which in the winter had sidewalks too icy to be walked on, dodging lorries rushing to and from the warehouse. The old corporate nature of the place dragged on progress, and box-ticking micromanaging anchored business decisions as well as artistic and editorial ones. I felt frustrated, craved momentum, and started to plan my exit.

After each day, despite the looming prospect of a long and draining commute, I relished the feeling of stepping into the lift and leaving. Closing the doors and taking the ride down to the ground floor was a rare moment alone after a day in a starkly lit open-plan office. Sometimes while inside I'd look at my reflection in the mirror. I saw it change over time, the fatigued reality catching up with the sallow wash of overhead lights. But no other part of leaving and getting home was as satisfying as those 15 or 20 seconds it took to ride the lift, not only because of the frustrating transport frequently subject to cancellations, through inhospitable industrial estate with sheet ice rendering pavements unusable in the winter, but because it was the part of the exit I had mentally assigned as the most meaningful. It was a ritualistic sigh of relief. It was the dividing line. I exited over and over again in that elevator and in my mind before the final, decisive exit at the end of my notice period.

One of my favorite job exits depicted on screen is really an entrance. (Or both at once.) *Mad Men*'s smart copy writer Peggy Olsen leaves her job, tired of being taken for granted and diminished by the men in the office. She strides down the corridor of her new advertising agency, holding a cardboard box of possessions, wearing sunglasses and smoking a cigarette. Her newfound confidence and success are palpable. When I carted my own cardboard boxes out, I thought of this scene, taking personal effects and myself out of the building for the last time. On my final day, I rode the elevator and took a picture of myself smiling in the mirror, then left by the front doors without looking back. Spring was just around the corner. I opened a miniature bottle of prosecco and drank from it with a straw then and there. Bubbles to match the levity of exiting once and for all.

Unlike glass elevators, which are often commercial fishbowls designed to be seen as much as seen from, most utilitarian elevators are dull and perfunctory, sometimes missing the presence and identity other reception areas are branded with. It's less common for corporate-led design to attempt to influence us there, leaving us alone with our thoughts, in between coming and going, entering and exiting, and floors themselves.

Glasgow

When I was growing up, I lived in a block of flats with only three floors, too small for an elevator. But some of my school friends lived in high-rises. Sometimes now when I am in an enclosed room such as a bathroom, with a vent but no windows, I get a rush of memory: something about the way the air whistles in, and the sensation of distance from life on the outside. It's a comforting feeling, a little suspended in time and place like hearing the sea in a shell, taking me out of myself and somewhere else, from memory.

Often the tower blocks were staffed by a concierge office and to get in required pressing a button on an intercom, then waiting for the electronic release of a heavy door and a rattling elevator up. Once inside, the views from the higher floors were always striking, high above the town with hills in the background showing there was more out there than our small domestic worlds. Nowhere else had access to those views, to see the town from the perspective of a bird.

Glasgow, where I live, is Scotland's most populous city, characterized by a grittier post-industrial heritage than the nation's capital Edinburgh (and arguably, certainly contentiously, a warmer spirit). The eviction and subsequent demolition of buildings known as the Red Road Flats is a tale of loss seeped into the local consciousness.

Large-scale disruption is familiar to Glaswegians. The M8 motorway runs right through the center of the city like a fast-flowing river, only at one short point parallel to the actual River Clyde. When the motorway was constructed in the mid-1960s, local communities, mostly working class, were displaced. Beautiful old Victorian buildings were knocked down in sacrifice to this monument to speed.

Because of the violence of its arrival, there are some infrastructure oddities in its vicinity, like the train station of Anderston, which sits under a motorway bridge roaring with cars. Accessed via winding walkways as though it were an island, it feels entirely out of place, and yet it was there first. I went through a phase of visiting the station, intending to go nowhere but to feel the sensation of exiting the doors into such an inhospitable, weird concrete landscape, against which humans look alien and uncertain. There's a particular motorway exit that veers off to the right in an elegant and smooth curve, sending cars flying between modern, glassy buildings of the financial district before depositing them straight into the city. The experience only takes around five seconds, but those seconds feel like Tomorrowland. Perhaps best of all, an exit abandoned in its construction for many years, left sticking up into the air and hanging there aimlessly, was known as the Road to Nowhere. Although blocked off from other lanes, to glimpse it was always with a shiver, imagining the possibility of accidentally driving off it. It contained the urban oddity and humor of Glasgow itself.

The Red Road development in the Balarnock outskirts of the city had already fallen in public perception some time before being declared unfit for habitation, dogged by crime, asbestos scares, and arson. The years of decline were tied strongly to poverty. It became a spot popular for suicide attempts, most sadly and infamously when a family of asylum seekers jumped together to their deaths in 2010 amid the hostile environment of Home Office asylum policy.[2] Upon its condemnation, residents were served with eviction notices, but not everyone wanted to leave. After all, it had been home to many, despite its problems, and emotional ties persisted in the local community, and in the 1990s it had been used to house refugees from Kosovo. Housing campaign and resident groups protested the demolition but were ultimately unsuccessful in halting it.

Demolition of the six tower blocks was staggered over time, an event on each occasion drawing crowds of local onlookers. In the run-up to Glasgow hosting the 2014 Commonwealth Games, a suggestion to blow up the last remaining tower as an opening ceremony novelty was met by fierce public backlash,[3] sensitive to the meaning the flats had for former residents, and the asylum seekers still housed in one final occupied building. That idea was quickly tossed in the wastepaper bin.

Ponte City

Exits are not always sudden. Sometimes they loom, and that can be just as restricting on where individuals can and cannot go. Exits can be slow and crumbling, chipped away at bit by bit.

One of the most notable examples of a tower block fallen in favor is Ponte City in Johannesburg, conceived in 1975 as a luxury high rise and marketed accordingly. In a South African city fractured by apartheid, this was code for white and wealthy. Ponte City's record for being the tallest residential skyscraper in Africa still stands.

> Ponte City was, once, a tower of dreams—a specific, Apartheid-era dream. The residential tower was first envisioned in the 1970s, at the height of Apartheid confidence and white Johannesburg's economic boom. Amidst the tower's 54 stories, the builders promised purpose-built bachelor pads (complete with raised bedchambers, offering dazzling views of the city), "Pallazzo-en-Paradiso" suites (flanked by meticulously screened off servant's quarters), and so many amenities—men's leisure wear outlets, sundecks, an indoor ski slope—that the tower's builders promised "Live in Ponte and never go out."[4]

At its base was a supermarket and social center called "Nucleus." J. G. Ballard's dystopian *High Rise*, a tale of psychological erosion in a similarly foreboding building, was published in the same year Ponte City opened. Built in a circular shape with a hollow interior—like rigatoni pasta standing on end in the pot—windows faced outward across the city fifty-five stories high. A proposal to use the building as a high-rise prison never came to fruition. The original cross sections of the plans look like View-Master slides, the next luxury room just a click away. At the very top of the building, towering over everything in the vicinity and seen from far away, shone the largest neon sign in the southern hemisphere, advertising brands like Coca-Cola; one literally looked up to it, and it was used as a navigating landmark from elsewhere in the city.[5]

From later, as the building was reimagined and redeveloped, are photographs of workers standing atop mountains of accumulated resident debris and garbage that filled the deep hollow core of the building several stories high, rather than being taken away by the city's sanitation services. Light shines in from above, and the small figures look to be picking their way through the natural wonder of a cave, in a rescue mission for the building itself.

Trash is rarely just trash. As cultural geography regularly insists, it is also often relational, resourceful, poetic even. It is, in short, a material of rich aesthetic and political value. But what of this relational geography is left when a space is cleaned up? What is lost? In Johannesburg, a city that has long prospered, spatially at least, through habitual cycles of rubbish and renewal, the impulse towards the sanitary has historically betrayed its tendency toward racial exclusion and erasure.[6]

Investors and developmental projects stopped and started to the rhythm of the mortgage crisis, and in the meantime, residents trying to live their lives became fodder for wider political and commercial agendas. In contrast to its auspicious beginnings, Ponte City became a byword for crime and poverty, notorious for gang activity. The building's shift from affluent white at its most luxurious to low-income black residents and squatters as it fell into disrepair tells a story of housing stability, race, and money. Rather than providing any kind of security, the building's solid, imposing structure was a kind of mirage. More recent pushes for clean-up, including renaming the structure "New Ponte," were revitalized in the wake of South Africa hosting the 2010 World Cup, and the sequence of financial impasse preventing deeply necessary renovation and sanitation was finally broken. New rules and security are said to have helped with security problems. Today's residents are a mix of races, middle and working classes, and there are programmed activities for children.

At the time previous residents were cleared out for these most recent renovations, photographer Mikhael Subotzky and artist Patrick Waterhouse amassed what is one of the most intriguing archives on large-scale eviction, moving focus away from the impactful building and glossy marketing materials and getting close to the lives of those within it.[7] As writer Darran Anderson described it,

As with the greatest science fiction, there is a paradoxical sense of the scene being simultaneously futuristic and ancient. Such a place must exist only in the realms of fiction; the fever dreams of Piranesi perhaps, Bentham's all-seeing Panopticon or the infernal industrial environment of Fritz Lang's Metropolis. The brilliance of Subotzky and Waterhouse's Ponte City series is that they demonstrate that this is only a shell for something more interesting and profound; the lives of the people who live there.[8]

Material gathered over several years, in the form of photographs, ephemera, advertisements, and interviews, is highly detailed. Abandoned papers and photographs show glimpses of residents who had already moved on. Some of Subotzky's photographs are intimate. A couple recline in a bath together. Children play in kitchens as parents attempt to corral them. As well as these atmospheric portraits of the residents' lives are methodical and almost obsessive cataloging of each and every doorway of the fifty-five stories. Some doors are painted, some decorative. Others have been rendered extra secure with the addition of bars and grills. Among this series of shots is the occasional resident standing in their doorway, wearing expressions ranging from welcoming to wary. The camera looks out of windows, too, showing what was seen by inhabitants who were soon to leave for somewhere else, among the city sprawl.

Like Mark Isaacs's project, here too are elevator shots with residents looking down at the camera, and in the context of eviction they take on new meaning. Many of those photographed would soon exit the building a final and decisive time, leaving it behind for good. Their routines and domestic comings and goings are frozen in time in the static images.

Accommodation informs health, family, community, safety, and security, but for many, the stability of where they live is dependent on wealth and control of capital, or the fluctuations of others' economic fortunes. When the threat of eviction looms, whether imminently or as a scenario of possibility in the future, residents have less grasp on the tangible world around them. In these instances, eviction notices are often unwelcome, or at least mixed, exit signs.

7 EVICTIONS AND EVACUATIONS

When thousands of people exit a place all at once, what gets left behind?

Kowloon Walled City

If Escher and Kafka had designed a city together, it might have looked a bit like Kowloon Walled City (KWC), the sprawling, densely populated settlement in Hong Kong—and that no longer exists.

Differing from what might typically be considered a city, Kowloon Walled City was strong in number, with 50,000 residents occupying a land mass of over six acres, at its peak 119 times denser than New York City,[1] and had a city's complexity within its walls. Unlike familiar city layouts with spaces in between architecture and infrastructure, KWC was one gigantic mass of conjoined buildings that developed intricately over time, adding layers atop layers—but no higher than fourteen stories because of close proximity to Kai Tok Airport, also a source of high noise pollution. Residents used the roof as a place for gathering, relaxation, and to source air and light.

The City's resident-constructed staircases, rickety bridges and labyrinthine, narrow passageways made it possible to traverse the upper floors of buildings without having to go down to ground level. How people move around cities (or buildings) has partially to do with the available infrastructure and planned access, and partially with spontaneously created routes. Inhabitants may wish to go from A to B by way of amenities or a route more aesthetically pleasing; they also react emotionally to the environment, to its familiarity, and to danger, real or perceived. As Jonathan Raban described in *Soft City*,

> the Piccadilly Line is full of fly-by-nights and stripe-shirted young men who run dubious agencies, and I go to elaborate lengths to avoid travelling on it. It is an entirely irrational way of imposing order on the city, but it does give it a shape in the mind, takes whole chunks of experience out of the realm of choice and deliberation, and places them in the less strenuous context of habit and prejudice.[2]

"Imponderabilia" is a performance piece by artists Marina Abramovic and Ulay,[3] in which a man and a woman stand naked on either side of a door frame. Visitors must squeeze past them. The physical stimulation, of closeness to another's nude body, prompts differing levels of comfort in participants. Bystanders may watch their facial expressions, judge how quickly or carefully they move between the two bodies, whether they go once or back and forth. Which way they turn, face to face with either man or woman. How difficult it is to pass through without touching the skin of other humans.

To go through a doorway draws metaphoric parallels with birth and death, but here what's important is the passage itself, not what's on the other side. The doorframe is the center of the artwork and its locus of meaning. Interacting with it may induce arousal, intimacy, curiosity, or embarassment. Participants may gravitate toward the bodies or be repelled by them. Whether viewed as an exit or entrance, what's important is making the shift from one place to another, into a new realm. Only by doing so do participants understand something about themselves.

By this point in my life, I've spent half of my years living away from my hometown. On a recent trip back walking through the town center, I felt the mental fuzz of disorientation, the contrast between deeply ingrained memories of routes and landmarks from my years living there, and how things have changed since, with shops, buildings, and station layouts changed. Or, to walk around a corner and find some sight—a small churchyard, a path—that I hadn't anticipated before spotting it, for it had faded from my mental map. I could feel a tension between old habits of route, and the route I now intended to take to get to my restaurant destination, confuse my senses and cause me to pause to look around several times. Strangest of all is that my high school was years ago demolished, replaced with a modernized building on a site across town. It was an eerie feeling to look at the empty space, other than a small protected front building still standing that was once the art department and used now for I don't know what. The gap left had been the location of so many strong and striking memories and a rush of visuals from heady, formative teenage years: intense friendships, feuds, romances, and plots. I had often been unhappy there but to think, this corridor, gone, that shortcut, gone, remaining only in the memories of people dispersed years ago—unexpectedly I felt sad. At the last moment before I was to walk past it, I turned impulsively and took a different street instead.

In KWC, residents shaped the social atmosphere of the city, as they do in other cities. In having such a high degree of control over the structure of the city itself, and the ability to make modifications over time to stairs and passageways, the residents molded the routes of their space as they wished, subject to available materials and the laws of physics.

Desire paths—where walkers choose to tread—are studied by city planners, and in Finland, tracks across the first snowfall of the year, not only visible to observers but at a time when existing routes would be covered over and so prompt more intuitive actions, have later been integrated into official park trails. KWC, like other slum housing, takes this principle into 3D, with routes created across vertical as well as lateral areas as residents traverse from building to building and modifications created directly by them without the input or boundaries of city planners or legislators.

It was said some rarely left the city, because so much could be found right there, although plenty of citizens living traditional lifestyles with jobs and schooling on the outside came and went each day. As well as being a law unto itself, it was also a world. Although sanitation and lighting sources were extremely poor, with reports of independently hooked up electrical connections sizzling dangerously, persistent leaking, and rats, there were also (unregistered) dentists, doctors, salons, churches, fishmongers, kindergartens, noodle makers, and manufacturing businesses, alongside more notorious sources of income like gambling and drugs. Distanced from health and safety codes, entrepreneurs flourished with law enforcement rarely intervening in anything but the most serious crimes. It was a city's worth of complexity, highly condensed, and contained tight knit social circles among residents.

As Sharon Lam has written about KWC:

> In my urban design paper, the Kowloon Walled City was brought up as an example of a "slum" that showed the consequences of the lack of building regulations. There was no mention of the delicious bowls of noodles one

could find there. Rather, the Kowloon Walled City is in conversation usually described as "post-apocalyptic," "scary" and "crazy." Compare this to the way in which my dad talks about the city—a smirk broke across his face as soon as the name was mentioned, and I was surprised to learn that his primary school was just next door from this "crazy" mass of drugs, gangs and crime. In fact, most of our conversation focused on the food that you could find there. […] He admits that he knew of people being mugged and that people generally avoided the place after dark, but otherwise my dad complimented the Triads on their organization of the Walled City. Acting as a de facto city council (albeit one funded by drugs and enforced through violence), the Triads organized a volunteer fire brigade and rubbish disposal, and resolved civil conflicts, particularly those between competing businesses.[4]

In the late '80s, the government began plans to evict residents and demolish the city, a topic of ongoing discussion amid diplomatic tension. *The Washington Post* reported at the time, "Despite British and Chinese claims of sovereignty, neither nation sought to police the Walled City for fear of causing a diplomatic incident. As a result, the area became a jurisdictional no man's land, a magnet for illegal immigrants from China and a haven for criminal activity."[5]

But eviction arrived suddenly one morning when police and authorities entered the City and began registering a total of around 33,000 individuals and many businesses. Eviction was long and slow, taking almost 2,000 days, and although compensation was offered resident resistance was strong, with organized anti-demolition committees and sometimes violent spontaneous protests along the way. For many who had lived their entire lives there, relocation and dismantling of the unique and independent culture of the City was unfathomable. The last 200 families remained until they were forced out. Demolition was completed in 1994, and where tens of thousands of people once stood, a park now occupies the site of Kowloon Walled City.

> One can say that the city itself is the collective memory of its people, and it is associated with objects and place. The city itself is the locus of the collective memory.
> —**ALDO ROSSI,** *Architecture of the City*[6]

With low-income groups typically underrepresented in literature and other media, the volume of aesthetic and dystopian romanticizations of Kowloon Walled City makes it an outlier once again, but what is really being depicted in these instances is not the true city, or its people, but a fictionalization, which doesn't aim to get to the heart of the place but build the concept of another place entirely with its detritus. Individuals who were never there have already formed their own memories of these simulated versions and have done so collectively through pop culture and entertainment moments entirely separately from their inspirational origin or people.

In instances of forced mass eviction, there is real danger that the social and cultural history of communities, particularly low-income and marginalized communities, will be erased or cast aside from conceptions of national history. The risk is also posed that individuals, feeling displaced from former homes which were embedded within rich and distinct communities, will experience feelings of insecurity in their ongoing conception of home and identity (as well as the strain of financial insecurity), compounded by lack of recognition of their previous locale in the general consciousness.

Forced evictions are rarely uncontroversial, with motivations ranging from benevolent improvement to commercial potential in underlying land, and rarely is it easy to re-house the huge populations of mass settlements. But when an exit is forced, instead of sought, compensation should extend to investment in the preservation of cultural memory.

Radical Cities

In his book *Radical Cities*, Jason McGuirk describes activist architecture of Latin American countries and instances of collective decision making in similarly low-income, high-density communities.[7] One example is Torre David, a tower block in Caracas, Venezuela, abandoned and unfinished after the financial crash, as is so often the backstory to crisis in property inhabitation. Taken up by squatters, an open-air atrium at the center became a space for participatory democracy, with residents taking their turn to speak and shape rules governing the 3,000 people who lived there. To the half-complete building, without elevators or windows, they introduced electricity, with a team of workers managing the mechanics. There was a water pump to distribute water to each floor, with limits on usage, and shops and services. It was unsafe by general standards, but it provided some of what was lacking to make a home, until the residents were forcibly evicted.

McGuirk highlights innovative architectural projects aiming to bridge the gap between slum communities and their integration with the wider bureaucratic city, finding ways to support resident-led ingenuity and existing communities without resorting to the wholesale displacement of residents. Of Medellin in Colombia, McGuirk notes,

> Until the early 2000s, government policies discouraged consolidating slums with staircases and transport infrastructure, because they were not supposed to be there. The mid-twentieth-century view that the slums were the 'cancer' to be cut out of the city resonated into the contemporary era, not least because they were an impediment to respectable development. Now, they are awarded some of the city's choicest buildings. Suddenly, the mutually exclusive agendas of social urbanism and urbanism of the spectacle can overlap, with a common goal.[8]

At the center of Medellin is a library: "The importance of the Biblioteca España is as a beacon, signalling to the city as a whole. There has been much derision of iconic architecture in recent years, but this building needed to be iconic. Its very purpose was to draw the gaze of prospering paisas to the hills that they had blinkered from view as if they didn't exist. The library has a symbolic purpose, which is to make the informal city visible."[9]

Nail Houses

All these examples show how exits are so often a class issue, and home ownership makes for a big difference between forced eviction and the choice to leave. In the case of real estate holdouts, having capital to bargain with is beneficial, particularly in the face of a corporation.

Beyond the principles of stability and security, there have been some famous and strange real estate holdouts. Edith Macefield became famous for turning down a million dollars for her home in the early 2000s, which stood in the path of a retail development that was ultimately built around her property and that looked even more quaint in contrast. Upon her death in the house at the age of 86, Disney publicists made the most of its likeness in the Pixar film *Up*, tying hundreds of balloons to its front gates, which prompted visitors from far and wide to do the same. (If there was a Disney store inside the mall, they probably did a good trade that day.) Other instances of homeowner stakeouts have also ended in marketing stunts. The Macy's corner building in

New York City, a backdrop beloved of Instagram influencers, and holding a prime real estate location, became known as the Million Dollar Corner after selling up for the sum on its eventual sale in 1911. In a show of commercialism marking its territory, the property is frequently decorated as a gigantic Macy's shopping bag.

When it comes to the balance of rights between individuals and corporations or individuals and the state not to have to exit their homes, some of the most fascinating and dramatic holdouts are in Asian countries experiencing periods of rapid infrastructure expansion with emerging economies. In China, these real estate holdouts are known as "nail houses," referring to the stubbornness of a nail that holds tight, sticking out awkwardly. Citizens have been permitted to own property since the 1990s, and the post-Communist economic boom in exploring this right has driven the development of new retail spaces, hotels, and other commercial centers in previously residential areas. But not every resident is prepared to move to make way for a mall, and with an awareness of quite recently bestowed rights, they don't have to.

While local officials could once order individuals off their land, a law was passed preventing government takeover—in most circumstances. There's still some dispute over a loophole where ejection can be forced when in the public interest, and what, exactly, that may mean in disputes between commercial developers and private property owners. In a young property market that is still finding its feet, owners made use of strengthened bargaining positions. Some nail houses have become legendary, particularly those most striking in their physical situation, like islands of one home amid seas of encroaching construction. In 2007, a homeowner was the last of his neighbors to refuse to move out of the way of a new six-story shopping mall. The developers responded by cutting his power and digging a massive, moat-like pit around his house. Eventually, the owners settled for a large financial sum, but not before planting a Chinese flag atop their precarious house. The phenomenon, however, has become a touchy subject, with reports that the film *Avatar* was dropped from distribution in China due to comparisons being made between nail houses and the film's theme of the relocation of indigenous people.

In many instances of societal instability, there is tension between individual rights and capitalist interests. Forced evictions often come down to money, or lack of it. Increasingly, the same is true of evacuation.

Climate Emergency

We are asking those in the potentially affected area who are power-dependent for medical reasons to use their own resources to get out. If they are unable to relocate and power loss will cause an immediate life threat, call 911 for transport to an Emergency Room.

—Tweet from @cityofberkeley in October 2019[10]

The next day, it was reported in the news that a man reliant on an oxygen tank died just twelve minutes after power was switched off. The official autopsy says it wasn't caused by the outage, but his family disagree.[11]

In the autumn of 2019, with temperatures beating historic records with each turn of a calendar page, the power company PG&E announced imminent city-wide power outages in Berkeley, California. The aim was to avoid exacerbating risk of wildfire. Fire departments had already asked residents to be careful if using any equipment that might cause sparks. Some residents evacuated until it all blew over. Others waited it out, walking through familiar routines in readying generators and stocking up on water, filling all available containers including bathtubs. In the days leading up to fires, there are always long lines at gas stations and supermarkets. Citizens grew concerned about those in their communities reliant upon health and mobility equipment powered by electricity, including elevators in buildings.

Like other emergency exit and evacuation scenarios, those with the means to facilitate their own removal ("their own resources") fare better on average. This is nothing new. Notoriously on doomed ship *Titanic*, lifeboats were a perk of higher paying passengers. The lower classes were housed in lower decks, most vulnerable to the danger that ultimately did unfold. This is only a more transparent example of how income, as well as age and health, impacts ability to evacuate.

What is novel are how privatized disaster services are attending to the wealthiest residents in the path of fire and flood. Money has always been made from disasters; the global climate crisis is no different. Sometimes such jobs aren't contracted by residents themselves, but by insurance companies keen to avoid bigger payouts. When Kim Kardashian's house was saved from wildfire,[12] many learned of the existence of private fire brigades for the first time. More of them are likely to crop up.

In Beyoncé's striking video for the song "Formation," the singer stands atop a police car sinking deep into flood water, recalling images of Hurricane Katrina and explicitly depicting black American experiences, heritage, and judicial injustice. It's an electric jolt of a song, speaking first and foremost to black women, celebrating one another and their collective strength, and it also brings criticism of inequality to the forefront of mainstream entertainment on the global stage. The handling of Hurricane Katrina was widely criticized for how New Orleans' population of lower income black families were disproportionately impacted. The gap between rich and poor is never more starkly apparent than in an emergency, when one's chances of escape are reliant upon available resources, not least in situations requiring evacuation. For those who find the everyday hard enough to afford, spending money in preparation for the possibility of a disaster in the future is beyond the finances of many individuals. Money and communities well invested in can mean many things in the event of a disaster, including greater access to communication and information before and after an event. Money is telephone costs, internet access, the cost of power even before it's switched off. Many shift workers do not have the ability to telecommute, with employers unsympathetic unscheduled leave. When it takes money to get out, in travel and accommodation, whole communities can and have suffered the consequences of underfunding and lack of investment in contingency planning.

In the event of the Grenfell fire tragedy in London in 2018, in which seventy-three died in a residential tower block, the social dividing lines contributing to the circumstances became clear. The concerns of residents, some of whom had explicitly warned disaster seemed likely, had been repeatedly brushed off; it turned out that the choice of cladding used in the building's construction had been a cheaper, highly flammable option.

One of the most enraging and saddening incidents of the aftermath encapsulated its gross injustice. Some surviving residents, many of whom had lost several family members, were housed in nearby accommodations. Homeowners of the more expensive properties complained their presence would bring down property prices, and objected to the children, who were recovering from the trauma, playing in the residence pool.[13]

> Two tiers of residents, two tiers of money. Two tiers of control over their immediate environments and existence within the city. Two tiers of life and death.

Class shapes our built environment just as it does our social one. The lights of some exit signs are switched on only for the wealthy. For others, more immediate and brutal exit signs threaten to come swift and unannounced, their possibility lingering always, in evictions, ejections, and evacuations.

Exits are a class issue, across money, race, bodies, and more. Exits and entrances mark out where we can and cannot go.

8 EXISTENTIAL EXITS

Exit as death, exit as birth. The circle of life depends upon clearly defined physical exits, which in turn resist existential clarity. It's no wonder humans mythologize them.

Spiritual journeys of many kinds, across many cultures, often end with an exit point upon reaching the end of terrible trials and tribulations, during which the subject proves their worth and fortitude. Bodies are almost broken before being reborn into a new realm, often heavenly. These ancient mythological journeys have modern legacy in the form of pilgrimage.

Writers across periods and regions have been fascinated with the journey to the underworld. In Greek mythology, deities set up camp at the entrance, along with terrible beasts. Their proximity underscores the link between physical departure and spiritual elevation. In many modern-day religions, burial and other ritualistic physical preparations of the deceased body are considered necessary to ensure good passage through the afterlife. Charon, who hung around Hades ferrying people to the entrance of the underworld, would turn away those souls who hadn't received a proper burial. Some tried to bribe him with a gold coin placed under their tongue.

In many cultures the dead are prepared according to ancestral tradition, with rituals born of religious belief carrying on and even absorbed by the non-religious. Graveyards are sites of remembrance long past the stage of decomposition; the site itself is considered meaningful, including when a gravestone is erected without remains underneath it. Sometimes flowers are left on decrepit stones which have seen no movement in many years by unseen strangers, one of the beautiful mysteries to be found in cemeteries and in the markers of mourning from decades and centuries ago.

There is much tender physicality in the observing of death. The weight of caskets straining shoulders. A handful of soil scattered by each attendee to give the casket its first covering. But we attach physical desires and needs to the dead themselves, with funerals maintaining rituals designed to help them on their passage beyond. Cold cheeks are kissed goodbye one last time, bodies are painted to give the impression of health. In Ancient Egypt, bodies were entombed, so as to be undisturbed, with items they night need in the afterlife, just as a favorite dram may be poured on a grave in libation. (Mine's a gin, thanks.) We touch ourselves to remind ourselves of the physical circumstances of a meaningful death: In Catholicism, worshippers touch areas of their body in order, representing the stations of the cross that pierced Christ's body; transubstantiation is the eating of his flesh and blood through Communion.

When my Papa died, I asked for a pair of his socks as a keepsake. I could picture him wearing them while sitting on his chair and smoking. When they got lost among the detritus of my room, balled up among all the other socks and completely resistant to my attempts to separate them, I tried to suppress the loss I felt because it felt like a smaller, second death, and worse—my own fault.

In contrast to what remains of ancient rituals marking death, digital rituals have recently emerged: alongside the now typical Facebook update, which in the wider Facebook universe sits alongside being able to mark oneself safe in a disaster or terror attack, there has been criticism of teens taking selfies with caskets or tweeting from funerals. This is often painted as inappropriate and evidence of self-absorption, but perhaps there is a healthy acceptance of death to be viewed in a younger generation, particularly one that encounters their own mortality in school shooter drills and awareness of ecological emergency, enveloping the instance of a loved one into the communicative norms of their everyday lives, even if the lifestyle of ongoing self-cataloging and immediate reaction has its own problems. In earlier days of internet connections before real names became de rigueur and it was easier to fall out of contact without a forwarding "address," there were death communication services, which would pass the message on to online friends, although it was dependent on a family member informing the service. Other than death, there are flourishing online worship services and all manner of other religious actions can be taken; over time these too will form their own rituals and color communication.

But for many, what we do with our bodies can be a primary way in which our spiritual selves are expressed. Purification rituals are also exits; the physical removal of dirt, perceived or present, from the exterior of a body may seem like more of a casting off rather than an exit, but it's a metaphor for ritualistic, spiritual cleansing, where what is problematic leaves our bodies. Do we become less spiritual when dirt appears on the body after ritual cleansing has purified us, or we leave a special site? We veer in and out of spiritual zones of being, mapped by the marking of rituals.

Around ten years ago I visited the Meiji Shrine in Tokyo, set within a large area of forested land in stark sensual contrast to the nearby Harajuku Station, outside which lace-bedecked Gothic Lolitas and other subcultures meet to show off their style, and nearby Takeshita Street, a wonderland of fast fashion, plastic gimmicks, and cute cafes. On an aerial map, the shrine is surrounded by a thick cushioning of lush green trees, separating it from a city filled with billions of lights. *Torii*, the large archways in Shinto culture, mark a transition from the mundane to the sacred. They're often placed on pathways or roads leading up to a shrine, and visitors may walk through several sets, each more sacred than the last, on their approach to worship. They can be seen in Japan, China, Thailand, and other East Asian countries. Some believe they originated in India, a theory centered around the torana gates at the Sanchi monastery, but this is thought largely to be conjecture based on linguistic similarity.

Upon walking through the large torii, as tall as the trees on either side of the path onwards, a calm descends. Thoughts of humidity and noise melt away. In the contemplative space I felt more conscious of my own breath within my body. I was visiting as a tourist, and keen not to do anything inappropriate or disrespectful, but simply to observe. I found instead I was affected by sense of peacefulness and hushed awe. Close to the central structure, there is a purification station called a *temiyuza*, a traditional font of water with wooden ladles. First, the left hand is rinsed, and then the right. The mouth is rinsed using the left hand, the left hand is rinsed once more, and the dipper is returned. An English translation on the official website provides a guide for tourists. Along with instructions for the routine to follow (illustrated with custom pictograms) and a request to preserve the dignity of this place, is a warning of mosquitoes.[1]

Exorcisms are an example of the body viewed as a conduit for evil, or a barrier to spiritual fulfilment; in them is the impetus to distance oneself from the flesh and its temptations, particularly those linked to sin, as is present in modesty garments and the scrutiny of women's appearance (which is often about the projection and rejection of inner temptations as much as it is about control). Here, exits are something internal, something to be gouged out from the inside in order to weaken the whole.

We create rituals for death, just as we do for life, as a way to understand and make our way through the experience. Many believe, or hope, that a send-off from the mortal world will be followed by an entrance to the afterlife. What happens there is beyond our knowledge; we grasp for physical effects and familiar words in guidance. It is comforting for some to imagine that nothing happens after death, that it is a peaceful finality, just as others believe in a heavenly (or hellish) place. But sometimes the door swings both ways, and an exit from the afterlife is possible, too. In Abrahamic religions, angels fall from Heaven having rebelled or sinned, tempting mortals. In Ovid's *Metamorphoses*, dog-like Cerebus was retrieved from the afterlife by Heracles and proceeded to vomit on the shores of Scythia, turning plants poisonous. Geographers of the myths have differing views on where, exactly, this took place. In Dante's *Inferno*, exiting Hell is possible by climbing down the physical body of Lucifer, continuing until the center of gravity shifts and it feels one is rising again.

It is no wonder that the exitscape of death has also fascinated artists.

> The way in which you quit it rewrote the story of your life in a negative form.
> **—EDOUARD LEVE,** *Suicide*[2]

Leve was a French photographer and writer whose short, literary works gleefully experimented with the boundaries between fiction and nonfiction and explored unconventional narration. In the book *Autoportrait* the narrator shares statement after statement about himself, encompassing both what seemed to be on the surface bland, factual, and often disparate (height, hair color, occupation) while gradually including subjective statements that cast doubt on the whole lot (e.g., stating his own attractiveness without couching it as opinion). The book played with stripping back the trope of the untrustworthy narrator—as well as the genre of autofiction, where stories are told through a self-conscious, stream-of-consciousness narration—to its bare and sparse parts.[3]

But Leve's most well-known work in his home country was *Suicide*. It also reeled off statements, but centered around a man who had committed suicide and was told in the second person, like memories being recounted. In one tragicomic episode, the dead man's wife had knocked over a comic book left open to a page thought to be his explanation for his death; once on the floor, the place had been lost before it could be read. Riffing off Perec, he said "I thought Life A User's Manual would teach me how to live and Suicide A User's Manual how to die."

Leve killed himself ten days after handing the manuscript to his editor.

It's not clear how much of the character was a creation, and how much he was based on Leve himself, compatible with his book's frequent interest in themes of self-depiction and doubt. If *Autoportrait* was a project of mythmaking through repetition, in *Suicide* Leve used the same format to come to a place of nullity, stripping back mystery line by line, just as the themes of both books are opposites, too, in life and death.

Academics have long been wary of biographical interpretations of texts. But Leve seemed to take pleasure in throwing this up in the air. It's a little like a joke, the ultimate blurring of boundaries, and induces readers to contend with external events that elaborate upon the book's themes. Despite the subject matter, his work feels clever and playful, rather than nihilistic.

We realize what no longer exists, just as we begin to grasp it, bit by bit.

9 EXIT THIS WAY

1. You are Evelyn McHale, who jumped from the Empire State Building's Observation Deck on May 1, 1947 and fell 86 stories. You had already exited this world when the photograph of your languid body on the roof of a glossy car, by chance suspended as though reclining and not dead, was described as "the most beautiful suicide." The note you left behind read "I don't want anyone in or out of my family to see any part of me. Could you destroy my body by cremation? I beg of you and my family—don't have any service for me or remembrance for me."[1]

2. You are a child in Victorian era England who has expired from [illness]. Your body is dressed in a starched smock with lace edging. In a quiet room your mother cradles you one final time, taking care to point your small face toward the photographer hidden under the cape of his machine. She surpasses the instinct to tremble, holding you in stiffened arms just as she holds the gaze of the lens. There are no portraits of you before life left your body but with this you

shall join the family album. The photographer presses the button. No more is expected of you.

3. You are a character in a console game, entirely respondent to player controls. In this level, there is a difficult-to-reach bonus item on a high shelf. The player is determined to get it, and instructs you to jump from a variety of positions. You run, and jump, and fall, and die. You run, and die in the pit below, too slow to jump to the next landmass. You jump and die over and over again, respawning each time. When the player gets frustrated, she quits without saving. There are other things to do, further to go, but you have exited play.

4. You are a flight attendant on the third domestic flight of the shift. As you wait for airport ground staff to affix staircases at either end of the plane, you alternate between looking straight ahead out of the window and smiling at the passenger first up to the door. He is a businessman waiting impatiently, itching to use his phone. Eventually your colleague opens the door and a fresh chill floods in, making everyone aware of how stale the air was moments before. You address thank-yous and good days to the departing backs of passengers gripping the rail.

5. You are lying stomach-down on your bed looking at college application brochures, considering whether you'll get the grades for programs you are interested in. It won't matter for another two years, but you like to look at the

forms anyway, imagining yourself one day receiving a letter in response. You've already rehearsed nervousness in the pit of your stomach on seeing it, the cinema slow-mo of picking it up, telling friends the news of your big move away. You hear doors being closed angrily in the kitchen down the hall and shove the brochures back under your bed, putting your headphones in.

6. You are wandering the neon-lit and rain-glossed paving of the entertainment district, accommodated in a nearby business hotel with evenings unplanned. Last night, you slept early, hungry but succumbing to jet lag. The further you walk, the less certain you are of where you began, but you navigate by impulse; the sounds of a gaming parlor are intriguing but the look from the man by the door discourages lingering. A little further on, you're handed a flyer with familiar food in unfamiliar words and your stomach guides your feet in search of a meal.

7. You have missed the motorway exit and must drive to the next one, cursing your second mistake within twenty minutes. Tiredness. You plunge one hand into a bag of chips nestled in a defunct CD rack and crunch them, licking the oil and salt off your lips. The next turn-off takes a while to come, and it'll double your journey time navigating the local roads back to where you intended to be. You feel pressure building in your chest, but swallow the upset, trying to get through a day where nothing is going right.

8. You are a Roborovski hamster being given the send-off you deserve. Wrapped in tissue inside a small box decorated tearfully with crayons and glue, held reverently in the hand of one who loved you. The smallest of all hamsters, you were a big personality, bigger than the sum of your parts. Your eyes are closed. Your nose is pink. Your almost weightless fluffy body is perfectly at peace. You are ready to join your predecessors in a small plot in the back garden, lowered down with solemnity and great care. It was a good life, and you will be remembered.

9. You are standing on the edge of a graveyard. The car is parked on the grassy verge of a quiet road, the door swung open as you left it, the action left hanging midway. It has been several years since last you visited, and protocol feels foreign, your body awkward. A breeze moves your hair back and forth as you look over the stones in the distance, but your cheeks are burning. You brought nothing, feeling awkward and embarrassed by not knowing what exactly was fitting, but now clutch the daffodils you found nearby, each pluck raining a scatter of dirt.

10. You are a bunch of burst balloons being shoved into a trash compactor, the detritus left over from a party a couple of nights ago. Having outstayed your welcome, one by one you were grabbed by the string and popped with a bent safety pin, deflating into splats of flaccid, formless rubber. Along with gift tags, gift bags, envelopes and wrapping paper,

stale cake, soda cans, paper plates and popped corks, your departure is a tumble of primary colors, cartwheeling down the dark, bumpy chute to the bin, a merry tangle of streamers and joy.

11. You are standing at the train door as it pulls into the station. You have, in fact, been standing here for a few minutes already, before all others still fiddling with bags in overhead racks. How hard is it to be prepared? The loudspeaker announces the station, reminding passengers to mind the gap on their exit from the carriage. You know all this already. Your finger is on the button first. You press it expecting doors to pop open immediately. When they don't, you grow agitated at the delay, jaw clenched. Three long seconds later, you are on your way, angry and indignant.

12. You're ready. Even though you know every last tin and packet down here, it's protocol to tick them off the list, and it reassures you to do so often. Beans, another kind of beans, powdered milk, aspirin, string . . . the medical case is a whole other list. To the right is the rack where you'll keep your gun. For now, it's on your hip at all times. When everyone else in the country takes leave of their senses, you'll be ready for the final days. You know it's coming and that's the difference between them and you. You pray for it every night.

13. You are one of the thousands of women who has disappeared or been found dead in Mexico in the last five

years. Your name has become a number. The number makes up the large total reported in foreign news articles. It's impossible to tell from a statistic what you were like. Whether you lived in fear or contentment; what made you laugh. What you would be doing, right now, if things were different. Of the femicides across the globe, yours is but one. A community group makes paper butterflies, to symbolize lives lost. They float away in the breeze.

14. You wait in the wings. The audience chattering has dipped in response to a change in music. They crane forward, looking for what they've spent their money on. You owe them. In these final moments, counting down with the beat for your cue to walk on boldly, you concentrate on stilling your heartbeat, breathing in and out slowly. You allow yourself the self-indulgence of recalling last night's applause. The curtains part and you walk into the light. All you can see is black, and your hand in front of you, waving to the cheapest seats up in the gods.

15. You see the little vanilla ice cream pot on the kitchen counter and feel sad she wasn't able to sleep last night. It wasn't there when you went to bed at midnight, when she was lying beside you trying to drift off. It's the evidence of an unquiet mind. She's sleeping now, sleeping in, but that's okay. You stand and watch for a moment before lying down beside her, putting your arm around her waist and breathing at her languid pace. Her mouth moves a little; she knows you're

there, but is too caught up to actually speak. You begin to drift away, too.

16. You are Henry I of England and you have eaten too many lampreys. The blood sucking, funnel-like, eel-shaped fish are rich and good to your palate, caught especially for your favor and their meatiness prepared in fine dishes amid the kitchen's bluster, banging, and heat. But: disaster. To your royal physician's concern, the pain in your gut is building. It cannot be stymied and the prognosis is bad. Eventually, you pass away. You died doing what you loved: eating lots of lampreys.

17. You stand on the threshold of miles and miles of raw American land. You have already journeyed a long way over similarly harsh terrain, but what lies in front is considered different altogether, although handfuls of the soil look the same. Different sections of different forms. Different dial codes. Different lives? On the horizon, there is no movement. The sun beats down. You take a sip from a battered water bottle. The others soon catch up with you. Together you press on, putting one foot in front of another, striving for the furthest point you can see.

18. You jump up into the cab of the truck with a muscle-familiar movement and it sets off before you can even swing the door closed. It's 4 a.m. and you'll perform the same movement many times again before the end of your shift,

hauling up bags of the city's garbage and guiding bin loads into the back of trucks, which sometimes leave you to go to the dump. Its replacement is trundling up the street while you catch your breath beside the curb. You like to look out for the grubby Mickey Mouse affixed to the grill of one of the trucks with cable ties. It makes you smile.

19. You are ground corn juddering down a conveyor belt inside a noisy action-packed factory. Eventually you'll puff up in the shape of a monster's claw, flavored and fried and sealed in bags. You could end up anywhere, on any supermarket shelf across the country. Now, in your raw state, all it takes is the right combination of pressure, water, and air, and you emerge from the extruder just right. Imitators try, but the hole is the most important piece of the puzzle. You're the correct and only shape, triumphant and golden, with just the right mouthfeel and crunch to satisfy consumer palettes.

20. You are an asparagus fern squatting in tasteful minimalist pottery. It's remarkable that your branches, so spindly and thin, can withstand any weight at all, but you grow in unexpected directions. Your owner, abreast of the latest fad for houseplants but ill-equipped for the responsibility, peers over your feather-like fronds, pale fresh green but browning at the edges. More water? Too much water? Sunlight? Less light? It's not clear. You are beginning to droop at the edges. You are not long for this world. Rot sweeps over your structure like rust, and no one around knows what you need.

21. You have missed your stop on the train. You come to this realization with a start, and again upon recognizing you were daydreaming of that last conversation. This is a comedy error. It's unlike you. At the next station, you depart and wait for a train back. It has been over a year, but you still wonder what it would be like to bump into him. To catch a glimpse through the window of buses travelling in opposite directions. Have you walked past one another unawares? Was it only you who was unaware? You half expect him to be on the platform but he never is.

22. You are many apples falling from an orchard's worth of trees. Plop, plop. Crunch.

23. You are beginning the voyage you have prepared for your whole life. Technically, you have prepared for this specific moment with specific technical exercises for the last two and a half years, and before that, a lifetime of dreams. You are suited up and it's thumbs up. All is in order. The hardest thing at this precise moment is staying calm as you exit the stratosphere, but you allow yourself a little giddy excitement. Your stomach is doing somersaults as the rockets blast for takeoff.

24. You are clicking the little x at the corner of the screen like you're meant to and nothing is happening for FUCK'S sake why has the program crashed again right when you're running out of time to get the stats into the presentation for tomorrow you're ALREADY on thin ice and this FUCKING machine won't do what you're telling it to why won't it CLOSE if it's BROKEN you just want out of this stupid crappy design of a system and back to the home screen but of course it's refusing to move and now your boss is coming over to ask how.

25. You are on the wait list for removal of the mesh implant. It was inserted into your vagina as a treatment for post-pregnancy incontinence, a full two years after concerns about the procedure first arose. It was meant to repair tissue but caused more harm. The mesh is now the subject of extensive discussion in the Scottish courts. It is not a comfort to hear politicians on television speak about this tiny piece of metal when they are so far away, and it is inside of you. The date is circled on your kitchen calendar. You want this thing out of your body.

26. You are about to cum. You feel a pressure rising from within. Your thighs are tense and shaking and you try not to think about the faces you are making. Fingers are working inside of you, three gesturing somewhere up high. Everything is already sodden—hands, sheet, face—when ejaculation rushes out of your vagina and gloriously down

your arm in three unpredictable gushes. Afterward, your laugh is on the verge of weeping. It feels like your nervous system is dissolving.

27. You are in the hospital bed that has held what little you weigh for almost two months. Your skin is translucent, stretched over the bones that have carried you many places throughout your life, some unexpected. Outside the sea swells in the distance, and some mornings you have requested to be wheeled over to see it when it is at its brightest blue, almost indistinguishable from the sky. Now, you are content with the memory. You grip your daughter's hand as she sits by your bedside. They are being brave for you, but you truly feel calm now.

28. You are six years old and have been in the care of an ICE detention center for sixty-three days while your case is pending, but you do not understand the words used by the adults who address you brusquely, or know that your grandparents are only a couple of miles away as the crow flies. They won't let you walk around outside of the bars that divide you and them, but you have grown used to that. You have stopped asking for anything because they do not respond. You sit more quietly every day, trying to become as small as possible.

29. You are a bear and your stomach is grumbling. Slowly you rise on four unsteady legs and shake your whole body,

hairs drifting off into the air. Blood makes its way back to your extremities. You flex a paw. Steps feel brand new. The familiarity of your heavy body comes back to you and you feel your mouth salivate with the thought of satiation. Nudging aside sodden leaves, you emerge into spring, blinking. You follow the path you already know, feeling the ruffling of your fur as you head down to the roaring river.

30. You are brand new, eyes closed, bawling you exit and the cord is cut and tied. You don't know who holds you, who passes you over to other hands, whose breast you rest on until a calm comes over you. Unfamiliar sounds. Unfamiliar smells. Your own unfamiliar self. You kick a foot, frog-like, testing the extent of it now free of the womb. When you open your eyes, shapes move in front of them. You don't know what you want or what to do until you're suddenly sucking, directed to the source of flowing milk, your first clue as to how to live in this world.

ACKNOWLEDGMENTS

Firstly, thank you to all at Bloomsbury and particular mention to Object Lessons editors Haaris Naqvi and Christopher Schaberg, for publishing these books that first inspired me, and taking a chance on my own.

A non-exhaustive list of those whose collective words of patience, kindness, support, encouragement, inspiration, commission, nonsense, and/or memes in the couple of years running up to and writing this book were helpful, in ways big and small, and whether they realize their contribution or not:

Oscar the Grouch, Leo Condie, Amanda Stanley, my Gutter magazine comrades Henry Bell, Kate MacLeary, Colin Begg, Calum Rodger, Ryan Vance, and Katy Hastie, my Tramp Press colleagues Sarah Davis-Goff and Lisa Coen, Sara Baume, my editor at *The Scotsman* Ian Johnston, Eve Livingstone, Claire Biddles, Ealasaid Munroe, Sasha De Buyl-Pisco, Nadine Aisha Jassat, Zeba Talkhani, Christina Neuwirth, Sim Bajwa, Beth Cochrane, Kirstyn Smith, Marion Sinclair and all at Publishing Scotland, Glasgow Women's Library, Zero Tolerance, Kirsty Logan, Heather Parry, Peggy

Hughes, Kaite Welsh, Gill Tasker, Lesley McDowell, Lara Williams, Kirstin Innes, Sara Sheridan, Fiona Brownlee, Richard Gillanders, Claire Strickett, Mark Macdonald, CJ Monk, Stephen McMahon, Andrew Gallix, Nathan Connolly, Michael Lee Richardson, Russell Bennetts, Houman Barekat, Rachel McCormack, Kathleen Caskie, Iain Robertson, Helen Archer, Jess Yuill, Sarah Higgins, Eilidh Lean, Ross Gillespie . . . and Beth, Jim, and James Waddell.

NOTES

Chapter 1

1. "Essex Lorry Deaths: People Found Dead Were All Vietnamese," BBC News, accessed November 10, 2019, https://www.bbc.co.uk/news/uk-england-essex-50268939.

2. A. Hay and L. Nicolson, "Deadly Crossing," Reuters, accessed November 18, 2019, https://graphics.reuters.com/USA-IMMIGRATION-ROUTE/0100818W2C4/index.html.

3. L. Paris, "Number of Migrant Deaths in Mediterranean Fell in 2018," NPR, accessed November 18, 2019, https://www.npr.org/2019/01/03/681956995/number-of-migrant-deaths-in-mediterranean-fell-in-2018.

4. Border Angels, accessed November 18, 2019, https://www.borderangels.org/about-us/.

5. Missing Migrants, accessed November 18, 2019, https://missingmigrants.iom.int/about.

6. S. Nebehay, "US has world's highest rate of children in detention— UN Study," Reuters, accessed November 18, 2019, https://uk.reuters.com/article/uk-un-rights-child/us-has-worlds-highest-rate-of-children-in-detention-un-study-idUKKBN1XS1R4.

7. Valeria Luiselli, *Tell Me How It Ends* (Minneapolis: Coffee House Press, 2017).

8. B. Cambria, Twitter, accessed November 18, 2019, https://twitter.com/BridgetCambria8/status/1190085065126100992.

9. B. Cambria, Twitter, accessed November 18, 2019, https://twitter.com/BridgetCambria8/status/1190087272701583361.

10. B. Cambria, Twitter, accessed November 18, 2019, https://twitter.com/BridgetCambria8/status/1190091581522632704.

Chapter 2

1. Jennifer Powell and Jutta Vinzent, *Art and Migration* (Chichester, UK: George Bell Institute, 2005), 14.

2. Powell and Vinzent, *Art and Migration*, 24.

3. Powell and Vinzent, *Art and Migration*, 24.

4. Magnus Hirschfeld, *L'Ame et l'amour, psychologie sexologique* [*The Human Spirit and Love: Sexological Psychology*] (Paris: Gallimard, 1935), preface.

5. Stefan Zweig, *Chess Story* (New York: New York Review Books, 2005).

6. M. Keun-Geburtig, "Irmgard Keun," Youtube.com, accessed November 18, 2019, https://www.youtube.com/watch?v=tDLglhQosLk.

7. Irmgard Keun, *Child of All Nations* (London: Penguin, 2009).

8. Michael Hofman, "Vernacular Dither," *London Review of Books*.

9. Stefan Zweig, *The World of Yesterday* (London: Pushkin Press, 2011), 251.

10 Suicide note of Stefan Zweig from February 22, 1942, accessed November 18, 2019, https://kuenste-im-exil.de/KIE/Content/EN/Objects/zweig-stefan-abschiedsbrief-en.html?single=1.

Chapter 3

1 "Primary education: a report of the Advisory Council on Education in Scotland," (Edinburgh: Scottish Education Department, 1946), 75.

2 Eimear McBride, Shakespeare and Company live recording, 2017, accessed November 18, 2019, https://soundcloud.com/shakespeareandcompany/eimear-mcbride-on-the-lesser-bohemians.

3 Sue Rainsford, "Beyond Modernism: Eimear McBride and Embodiment," 2017, Ploughshares, accessed November 18, 2019, http://blog.pshares.org/index.php/beyond-modernism-eimear-mcbride-and-embodiment/.

4 Kenya Hara, *White* (Baden: Lars Mueller Publishers, 2019), 74.

5 Helen Adam 1909–1993, Scottish Poetry Library, accessed November 18, 2019, https://www.scottishpoetrylibrary.org.uk/poet/helen-adam/.

6 Kristin Prevallet, "The Worm Queen Emerges," in *Girls Who Wore Black: Women Writing the Beat Generation*, ed. Ronna Johnson and Nancy McCampbell Grace (New Brunswick, NJ: Rutgers University Press, 2002), 35.

7 W. Packard, "Interview with Adam," *New York Quarterly* 21 (Winter 1978): 13–23.

8 Helen Adam, "The Fair Young Wife," accessed November 18, 2019, https://www.scottishpoetrylibrary.org.uk/poet/helen-adam/.

9 Prevallet, "The Worm Queen Emerges," 2002, 37.

10 Helen Adam, "After Listening to Allan Ginsberg," in *A Helen Adam Reader*, ed. Kristen Prevallet (Orono, ME: National Poetry Foundation, 2007).

11 Hara, *White*, 16.

12 Anaïs Nin, *Incest: From A Journal of Love: The Unexpurgated Diary of Anaïs Nin 1932–1934* (New York: Harcourt Brace Jovanovich, 1972).

13 Anaïs Nin, *Henry and June* (London: Penguin Modern Classics, 2001), 167.

14 Nin, *Henry and June*, 232.

Chapter 4a

1 Louis Waldman, *Labor Lawyer* (New York: E.P. Dutton, 1944), 32–33.

2 Rose Schneiderman, "We Have Found You Wanting," in *Out of the Sweatshop: The Struggle for Industrial Democracy*, ed. Leon Stein (New York: Quadrangle/New Times Book Company, 1977), 196–97.

3 David Rosner and Gerald Markowitz, "The Early Movement for Occupational Safety and Health," in *Sickness and Health in America*, ed. Judith Walzer Leavitt and Ronald L. Numbers (Madison: University of Wisconsin Press, 1997), 475.

Chapter 4b

1. Paul Mijksenaar and Piet Westendorp, *Open Here: The Art of Instructional Design* (London: Thames & Hudson, 1999), 41.

2. Manfredo Massironi, *The Psychology of Graphic Images* (London: Lawrence Elbaum Associates Publishers, 2002), 265.

3. Massironi, *The Psychology of Graphic Images*, 260.

4. Paul E. Teague and Chief Ronald R. Farr, "Case Histories: Fires Influencing the Life Safety Code," in *Life Safety Code Handbook*, accessed November 18, 2019, https://www.nfpa.org/~/media/Files/forms%20and%20premiums/101%20handbook/NFP101HB09_CHS1.pdf.

5. accesibleexitsigns.com, accessed November 18, 2019, https://accessibleexitsigns.com/signs/combined-accessible-means-of-egress-icon-and-running-man-exit-sign-options/.

6. "Accessible Means of Egress Icon," egressgroup.net, accessed November 18, 2019, https://egressgroup.net/accessible-means-of-egress-icon/.

Chapter 4c

1. Michiko Kakutani, *The Death of Truth* (London: HarperCollins, 2017), 105.

2. Jenny Holzer website, https://projects.jennyholzer.com.

3. Jenny Holzer, *It is Guns* installation, https://projects.jennyholzer.com/it-is-guns/new-york/gallery.

4. "Exit" playlist compiled by Jordon Luc, YouTube, accessed November 18, 2019, https://www.youtube.com/playlist?list=PLX9Nj9VBKuUgypPekFA0Xi0D8ysR_avLz.

Chapter 5

1. J. Read, "Boris Johnson appears to finally admit his '£350m a week' claim was wrong," *New European*, accessed November 18, 2019, https://www.theneweuropean.co.uk/top-stories/boris-johnson-350-million-a-week-nhs-claim-1-6264572.

2. Yes campaign design, yes.scot, accessed November 18, 2019, https://www.yes.scot/app/themes/itstime/dist/images/logo.svg.

3. J. Elgott, "Theresa May Calls for Red White and Blue Brexit," *The Guardian*, accessed November 18, 2019, https://www.theguardian.com/politics/2016/dec/06/theresa-may-calls-for-red-white-and-blue-brexit.

4. J. Henley, "Project Fur: Dutch Unveil Big Blue Brexit Monster," *The Guardian*, accessed November 18, 2019, https://www.theguardian.com/politics/2019/feb/14/project-fur-brexit-is-a-big-blue-monster-say-the-dutch.

5. Rebecca Solnit, *Call Them by Their True Names* (London: Granta, 2018), 9.

6. Hannah Arendt, *The Origins of Totalitarianism* (Cleveland, OH: Meridian Books, 1958), 474.

7. A. Cowburn, "Theresa May says 'Brexit Means Brexit,'" *Independent*, accessed November 18, 2019, https://www.independent.co.uk/news/uk/politics/theresa-may-brexit-means-brexit-conservative-leadership-no-attempt-remain-inside-eu-leave-europe-a7130596.html.

8. "Exit," *Sesame Street*, 1974, accessed November 18, 2019, https://www.youtube.com/watch?v=3dFYsrGw5eI.

9. "Exit," *Sesame Street*, 1992, accessed November 18, 2019, https://www.youtube.com/watch?v=eibU_Sajbtg.

10 "Grover Explains Exit," *Sesame Street*, 2010, Available online accessed November 18, 2019, https://www.youtube.com/watch?v=IRQmsSVdpsY.

11 "Exit," *Sesame Street*, 1980, accessed November 18, 2019, https://www.youtube.com/watch?v=ncwiNq9jYOU.

12 "I Love Trash" in "40 Years of Sunny Days," *Sesame Street*, accessed November 18, 2019, https://www.youtube.com/watch?v=rxgWHzMvXOY.

13 Tweet by Twitter user @jamcolley on 18 Feb 2018, accessed November 18, 2019, https://twitter.com/JamColley/status/965044450182414336.

14 "Oscar Teaches Slimey How to Cross The Road," *Sesame Street*, 1981, accessed November 18, 2019, https://www.youtube.com/watch?v=O-eVO8bsmwI.

15 Adam, "After Listening to Allan Ginsberg."

16 @binanimals, Twitter, accessed November 18, 2019, https://twitter.com/binanimals.

17 L. Stack, "A Giant Bird Killed Its Owner. Now It Could be Yours," *New York Times*, accessed November 18, 2091, https://www.nytimes.com/2019/04/24/us/cassowary-bird-florida.html.

18 Fiona Tan, "Disorient," video installation, https://fionatan.nl/project/disorient/.

19 M. Howie, "Malaysia says it will not become a dumping ground for rich Western nations," *Evening Standard*, accessed November 18, 2019, https://www.standard.co.uk/news/world/malaysia-says-it-will-not-become-a-dumping-ground-for-rich-western-nations-a4152601.html.

20 G. Butler, "Men Don't Recycle Because They Don't Want People Thinking They're Gay, Study Finds," Vice, accessed

November 18, 2019, https://www.vice.com/en_au/article/j5ye73/men-dont-recycle-because-dont-want-people-thinking-theyre-feminine-gay-study.

21 Twitter user @no1guncle, Twitter, accessed November 18, 2019, https://twitter.com/no1guncle/status/1158741048400760832.

22 "Man ordered to collect fridge he threw off Spanish cliff," BBC, accessed November 18, 2019, https://www.bbc.co.uk/news/world-europe-49248764.

Chapter 6

1 Mark Isaacs, *Lift* (2001), accessed November 18, 2019, https://www.youtube.com/watch?v=FJNAvyLCTik.

2 K. Scott, R. Booth, and L. Harding, "Red Road Deaths: a tragedy of asylum, mental health and Russian intrigue," *Guardian*, accessed November 18, 2019, https://www.theguardian.com/uk/2010/mar/12/red-road-deaths-russian-asylum-seekers.

3 B. Ferguson, "Blow up Red Road flats? Gonnae no dae that?" *Scotsman*, accessed November 18, 2019, https://www.scotsman.com/news-2-15012/blow-up-red-road-flats-gonnae-no-dae-that-1-3367118.

4 A. Strecker, "Ponte City: A Portrait of Johannesburg," in LensCulture, accessed November 18, 2019, https://www.lensculture.com/articles/mikhael-subotzky-ponte-city-a-portrait-of-johannesburg.

5 Matthew Burbridge, "Ponte says yebo to new neon sign," IOL, accessed February 12, 2020, https://www.iol.co.za/news/south-africa/ponte-says-yebo-to-new-neon-sign-34200.

6. Ed Charlton, "Trashing Johannesburg: Ponte City-as-archive of everyday loss," London School of Economics Research (2019), http://eprints.lse.ac.uk/101462/.

7. Michael Subotzky and Patrick Waterhouse, *Ponte City* (Gottingen: Steidl, 2014).

8. Darran Anderson, "Ponte City," Magnum Photos, accessed November 18, 2019, https://www.magnumphotos.com/arts-culture/society-arts-culture/mikhael-subotzky-ponte-city/.

Chapter 7

1. C. Weller, "Kowloon Walled City in Hong Kong was 119 Times as Dense as New York," *Independent*, accessed November 18, 2019, https://www.independent.co.uk/travel/hong-kong-kowloon-walled-city-greg-girade-renegade-photographer-new-york-city-a7845111.html.

2. Jonathan Raban, *Soft City*, (London: Hamish Hamilton, 1974), 162.

3. Marina Abramovic and Ulay, *Imponderabilia*, performance piece.

4. Sharon Lam, "Here's What Western accounts of the Kowloon Walled City Don't Tell You," ArchDaily, accessed November 18, 2019, https://www.archdaily.com/800698/heres-what-western-accounts-of-the-kowloon-walled-city-dont-tell-you.

5. D. Deane, "Hong Kong Begins Effort to Clear Walled City Slum," *Washington Post*, accessed November 18, 2019, https://www.washingtonpost.com/archive/politics/1991/11/29/hong-kong-begins-effort-to-clear-walled-city-slum/8a714cb8-5413-4f46-bb9c-5d73e827d311/.

6 Aldo Rossi, *The Architecture of the City* (Cambridge, MA: MIT Press, 1984), 130.

7 Justin McGuirk, *Radical Cities* (ebook edition, London: Verso, 2017).

8 McGuirk, *Radical Cities*, 374.

9 McGuirk, *Radical Cities*, 474.

10 Tweet from user @CityofBerkeley, October 9, 2019, accessed November 18, 2019, https://twitter.com/cityofberkeley/status/1182060341129179137?lang=id.

11 P. McGreevy, "Man, 67, died 12 minutes after PG&E cut power, but autopsy says outage wasn't the cause," *Los Angeles Times*, accessed November 19, 2019, https://www.latimes.com/california/story/2019-10-11/pge-power-outage-elderly-man-autopsy-heart-disease.

12 Alexis C. Madrigal, "Kim Kardashian's Private Firefighters Expose America's Fault Lines," *Atlantic*, accessed November 18, 2019, https://www.theatlantic.com/technology/archive/2018/11/kim-kardashian-kanye-west-history-private-firefighting/575887/.

13 M. Chandler, "Outrage as luxury flat residents complain rehomed Grenfell tower families will lower house prices," *Evening Standard*, accessed November 18, 2019, https://www.standard.co.uk/news/london/outrage-as-luxury-flat-residents-complain-rehomed-grenfell-families-will-lower-house-prices-a3570331.html.

Chapter 8

1 "Your Shrine Visit," meijijingu.or.jp, accessed November 18, 2019, http://www.meijijingu.or.jp/english/your/1.html.

2 Edouard Leve, *Suicide* (Paris: Editions Gallimard, 2004), 29.

3 Edouard Leve, *Autoportrait* (Dublin: Dalkey Archive Press, 2002), 5.

Chapter 9

1 https://en.wikipedia.org/wiki/Evelyn_McHale, accessed November 19, 2019.

INDEX

1964 Olympics   42
2010 World Cup   92
2014 Commonwealth
     Games   89

Abramovic, Marina   96–7
Accessible Exit Sign Project,
     Australia   48, 49
*Action Against the Un-German
     Spirit* campaign   13
Acts of Union (1707), UK   19
Adam, Helen   5, 23–5
airports   58–9
algorithms   2, 5, 6, 9
Anderson, Darran   92–3
Anderson, Wes   15
Architecture of the City
     (Rossi)   101
Arendt, Hannah   71
Argentina   62
Arizona   5
Autoportrait (Leve)   117

Ballard, J. G.   90–1

Basel Convention (2020)   77
Bauhaus   12
Beats   23
Becker, Paula Moderson   12
Berkeley, California   106–7
Beyoncé   108
Blensdorf, Ernst   10
Blue Purple Tilt (Holzer)   63
books and publishing   85
     readers   27–30
Border Angels   4
Brecht, Bertolt   13
Brexit movement, UK   60,
     67–71, 73
Broad City, TV series   xiv
Brutalism   82
Burns, Robert   19–20

Cambria, Bridget   6–7
CCTV *see* closed-circuit TV
     (CCTV)
Cerf, Chris   71–2
CGI *see* computer-generated
     imagery (CGI)

Chess Story (Zweig)   14
Child of All Nations (Keun)   15
China   62, 77, 105–6
closed-circuit TV (CCTV)   56
Communist Party   11, 105
computer-generated imagery (CGI)   62

Dada   10, 12
Dante   116
death rituals   112–13, 116–18
Degenerate Art Exhibition, Munich, Germany (1937)   11, 13
digital rituals   113–14
"Disorient" (Tan)   77
Dix, Otto   12

Eastman, Crystal   36
easyJet   53
Egress Group   49
emigration/immigration   2–5, 100, 101–2
    in arts and culture   6, 12–17, 25
    children   5–7
    workers   31–4
emojis   43
    see also pictograms
Ernst, Max   12
Escher, M. C.   95

European Union (EU)   67, 69
eviction   95–6, 100–2
Exhibition of Twentieth Century German Art (1938)   12
"Exit" (Cerf, Stiles)   71–2
exorcisms   115
Expressionism   12

Factory Investigating Commission, New York   37
"Fair Young Wife, The" (Adam)   24
Finland   98–9
"Formation" (Beyoncé)   108
Freud, Sigmund   13

GAATES *see* Global Alliance on Accessible Technologies and Environments (GAATES)
Gaelic   20
garbage and environmentalism   75–9, 91–2
Garfield   74
Ginsberg, Allen   24
Global Alliance on Accessible Technologies and Environments (GAATES)   48–9
Goebbels, Joseph   9

INDEX   145

Gove, Michael 60
Grand Budapest Hotel, The (Anderson) 15
Greek mythologies 111–12
Greenpeace 78
Grenfell fire, London, UK 109
Groscz, George 12
Grover 72

Hara, Kenya 22–3, 27
Haring, Keith 72
Henry I, King of England 125
Hesse, Hermann 13
High Rise (Ballard) 90–1
Hirschfeld, Magnus 13
Hitler, Adolf 15
Hofman, Michael 15–16
Holzer, Jenny 63–4
homelessness 102–3
home ownership individuals *vs.* corporations 104–6
Hurricane Katrina 108

IKEA 57–8
"Imponderabilia" (Abramovic, Ulay) 96–7
Incest (Nin) 29
Inferno (Dante) 116
Instagram 105

Institut für Sexualwissenschaft (Institute of Sex Research) 13
International Organization for Standardization (ISO) 47, 49
internet and social media 26–7, 43, 59–60, 61, 75–9, 105
Ireland 20, 21–2
Isaacs, Mark 81–5, 93
ISO *see* International Organization for Standardization (ISO)

Japan 22–3, 42, 43–4

Kafka, Franz 95
Kai Tok Airport, Hong Kong 96
Kardashian, Kim 108
Keun, Irmgard 14–15
Keun-Geburtig, Martina 15
Kirchner, Ludwig 12
Kowloon Walled City, Hong Kong (KWC) 95–6, 98–101

labor movement 35–7
Ladies' Garment Workers' Union 35
Lam, Sharon 99–100
Latin America 102–4

Le Corbusier 82
Leve, Edouard 116–18
Lift (Isaacs) 81–5
LoCos pictorial language (Oto) 44–5
London Underground, UK 42
Luiselli, Valeria 5–6

McBride, Eimear 21–2
MacDiarmid, Hugh 23
Macefield, Edith 104
McGuirk, Jason 102–4
McHale, Evelyn 119
Macy's, New York City 104–5
Mad Men, TV series 86
Mary Queen of Scots 13–14
May, Theresa 69–70, 71
Medellin, Colombia 103–4
Meiji Shrine, Tokyo, Japan 114–15
Metamorphoses (Ovid) 116
Mexico 5–6, 123–4
Missing Migrants Project 4
Morgan, Edwin 23–4
Mortimer, Raymond 12
Museum of Modern Art, New York City 49
Mussolini, Benito 15

nail houses 105–6
Naropa Institute, Boulder, Colorado 24

National Health Service (NHS), UK 68, 69
Nazis 9–17
New Burlington Galleries, London, UK 12
New Orleans, Louisiana 108
New Sachlichkeit 12
New York City 31–7
NHS *see* National Health Service (NHS), UK
Nin, Anaïs 29

Oscar the Grouch 73–4
Oto, Yukio 43–5
Ovid 116

Pacific Gas and Electric (PG&E) 107
pictograms 42–3, 44–5, 49
Ponomarev, Sergey 6
Ponte City, Johannesburg, South Africa 90–4
Prevallet, Kristin 24–5
purification rituals 114–15

Raban, Jonathan 96
Radical Cities (McGuirk) 102–4
Rainsford, Sue 21–2
Red Road Flats, Glasgow, Scotland 88–9

INDEX **147**

Reichskulturkammer (Reich Culture Chamber) 10, 11, 14
Roborovski hamsters 122
Romantic movement 24
Rossi, Aldo 101
Royal Game, The (Zweig) *see Chess Story* (Zweig)

San Francisco, California 23
Schlemmer, Oskar 12
Schneiderman, Rose 35–6
Scotland 68–9, 97–8
  Glasgow 87–9
  Scots language 19–25
  Scottish independence movement 68, 69
Second World War 47
Sesame Street, TV series xiv, 71–5
Shinto 114
signs
  accessibility 48–9, 52–3, 59, 96–100
  adaptability 55–66
  arts and culture xv, 9–17, 22–30, 45–6, 63–4, 71–5, 81–5, 96–7, 108
  clarity xvi, 39–53, 55–66
  class and money 106–10
  design xvi, 39–53, 57–9, 61
  emergencies 39, 106–10
  and environment 49–51, 61, 63
  eviction 90–4, 95–6, 100–2, 104–6
  exits 119–30
  exploitation and hacking 64–6
  fantasies xiii–xv, 29–30
  freedom xv, xvii, 27, 29–30
  illumination xiii–xiv, 49–51, 56–67, 109–10
  internet and social media 26–7, 59–60, 61, 75–9, 105
  language 1–2, 19–22
  legislation xvi, 5, 37, 41, 43, 46, 99
  monitoring 55–66
  motorways 88–9
  movement 96–100
  pictograms 42–3, 44–5, 49
  politics and protests 5, 9–17, 35–7, 60, 67–71
  promise xiv, xvii, 22–3
  safety and security xvi, 31–4, 37–8, 40–3, 48–53, 55–66, 106–10
  sociability 99–100
  social history 31–4, 101–2
  standardization 37, 43–4, 47–9

technology 48, 49–53, 55–66
usage 45–6
snawplough 21, 22
Soft City (Raban) 96
Solnit, Rebecca 70
Soviet Union 44
spiritual journeys 111–18
Stiles, Norman 71–2
Subotzky, Mikhael 92–3
Suicide (Leve) 116, 117–18
Surrealism 10, 12

Tan, Fiona 77
Tell Me How It Ends (Luiselli) 5–6
Titanic 107
torii 114–15
Torre David, Caracas, Venezuela 102–3
Triangle Shirtwaist Company fire, New York City 31–4, 37, 41, 48
Trump Tower, New York City 64

Twilight Zone, TV series 2
Twitter 65

Ulay 96–7
United Nations (UN) 4, 5, 47
Up (Docter) 104
Uprising of 20,000, New York City 35
US Border Patrol 4

Victoria Hall disaster, Sunderland, UK 37
Vietnam 4

Waldman, Louis 33–4
Washington Post 100
Waterhouse, Patrick 92–3
White (Hara) 22–3
Workers' Compensation Act 37

Yeo Bin Yee 77–8
YouTube 59–60, 65–6

Zweig, Stefan 12–14, 15–17

OBJECT LESSONS

Cross them all off your list.

political sign	**gin**	**snake**
9781501358104	9781501353277	9781501348716
bulletproof vest	**coffee**	**environment**
9781501353024	9781501344350	9781501361906

"Perfect for slipping in a pocket and pulling out when life is on hold."
– *Toronto Star*

bird	**cell tower**	**compact disc**
9781501353352	9781501348815	9781501348518
ocean	**high heel**	**hood**
9781501348631	9781501325991	9781501307409

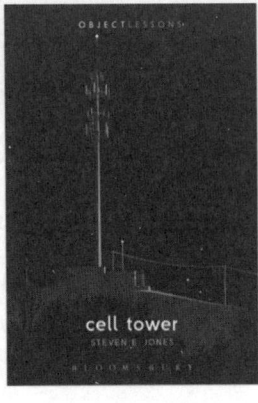

Burger by Carol J. Adams

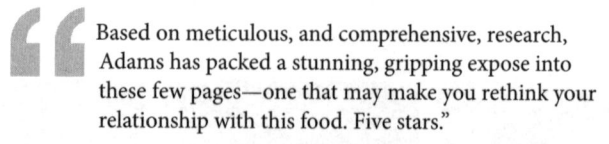

> Based on meticulous, and comprehensive, research, Adams has packed a stunning, gripping expose into these few pages—one that may make you rethink your relationship with this food. Five stars."
>
> *San Francisco Book Review*

> Adams would seem the least likely person to write about hamburgers with her philosophically lurid antipathy to carnivory. But if the point is to deconstruct this iconic all-American meal, then she is the woman for the job."
>
> *Times Higher Education*

> It's tempting to say that *Burger* is a literary meal that fills the reader's need, but that's the essence of Adams' quick, concise, rich exploration of the role this meat (or meatless) patty has played in our lives."
>
> *PopMatters*

High Heel by Summer Brennan

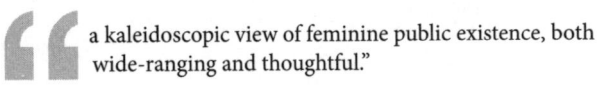

> a kaleidoscopic view of feminine public existence, both wide-ranging and thoughtful."
>
> *Jezebel*

> Brennan makes the case that high heels are an apt metaphor for the ways in which women have been hobbled in their mobility. She also tackles the relationship between beauty and suffering, highlighting the fraught nature of reclaiming objects defined under patriarchy for feminism."
>
> *Paste Magazine*

> From Cinderella's glass slippers to Carrie Bradshaw's Manolo Blahniks, Summer Brennan deftly analyzes one of the world's most provocative and sexualized fashion accessories . . . Whether you see high heels as empowering or a submission to patriarchal gender roles (or land somewhere in between), you'll likely never look at a pair the same way again after reading *High Heel*."
>
> *Longreads*

> "Brennan's book, written in very small sections, is short, but powerful enough to completely change your world view."
>
> *Refinery29*

> "In *High Heel*, the wonderful Summer Brennan embraces a slippery, electric conundrum: Does the high heel stand for oppression or power? . . . *High Heel* elevates us, keeps us off balance, and sharpens the point."
>
> *The Philadelphia Inquirer*

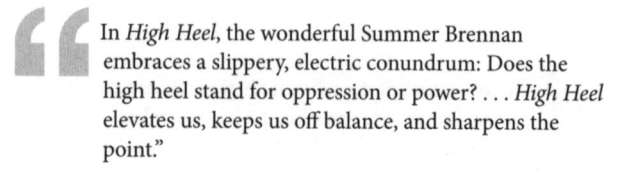

Hood by Alison Kinney

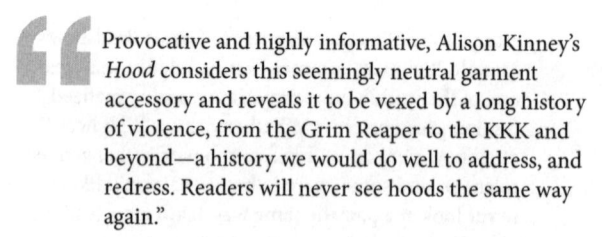

> "Provocative and highly informative, Alison Kinney's *Hood* considers this seemingly neutral garment accessory and reveals it to be vexed by a long history of violence, from the Grim Reaper to the KKK and beyond—a history we would do well to address, and redress. Readers will never see hoods the same way again."
>
> Sister Helen Prejean, author of *Dead Man Walking*

Hood is searing. It describes the historical properties of the hood, but focuses on this object's modern-day connotations. Notably, it dissects the racial fear evoked by young black men in hoodies, as shown by the senseless killings of unarmed black males. It also touches on U.S. service members' use of hoods to mock and torture prisoners at Abu Ghraib. Hoods can represent the (sometimes toxic) power of secret affiliations, from monks to Ku Klux Klan members. And clearly they can also be used by those in power to dehumanize others. In short, *Hood* does an excellent job of unspooling the many faces of hoods."

Book Riot

[*Hood*] is part of a series entitled Object Lessons, which looks at 'the hidden lives of ordinary things' and which are all utterly 'Fridge Brilliant' (defined by TV Tropes as an experience of sudden revelation, like the light coming on when you open a refrigerator door).... In many ways *Hood* isn't about hoods at all. It's about what—and who—is under the hood. It's about the hooding, the hooders and the hoodees ... [and] identity, power and politics.... Kinney's book certainly reveals the complex history of the hood in America."

London Review of Books

Personal Stereo by Rebecca Tuhus-Dubrow

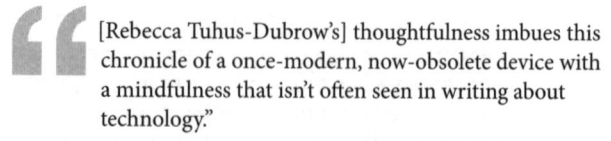

> [Rebecca Tuhus-Dubrow's] thoughtfulness imbues this chronicle of a once-modern, now-obsolete device with a mindfulness that isn't often seen in writing about technology."
>
> *Pitchfork* (named one of *Pitchfork*'s favorite books of 2017)

> After finishing *Personal Stereo*, I found myself wondering about the secret lives of every object around me, as if each device were whispering, 'Oh, I am much so more than meets the eye' . . . Tuhus-Dubrow is a master researcher and synthesizer. . . . *Personal Stereo* is a joy to read."
>
> *Los Angeles Review of Books*

> *Personal Stereo* is loving, wise, and exuberant, a moving meditation on nostalgia and obsolescence. Rebecca Tuhus-Dubrow writes as beautifully about Georg Simmel and Allan Bloom as she does about Jane Fonda and Metallica. Now I understand why I still own the taxicab-yellow Walkman my grandmother gave me in 1988."
>
> Nathaniel Rich, author of *Odds Against Tomorrow*

> [A] careful, astute study."
>
> *The Wire*

Souvenir by Rolf Potts

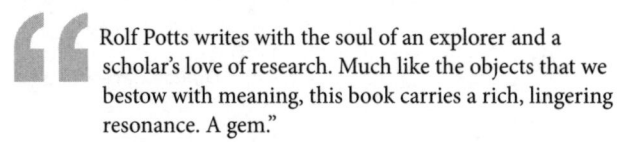

> Rolf Potts writes with the soul of an explorer and a scholar's love of research. Much like the objects that we bestow with meaning, this book carries a rich, lingering resonance. A gem."
>
> Andrew McCarthy, actor, director, and author of
The Longest Way Home (2013)

> *Souvenir*, a sweet new book by Rolf Potts, is a little gem (easily tucked into a jacket pocket) filled with big insights . . . *Souvenir* explores our passions for such possessions and why we are compelled to transport items from one spot to another."
>
> *Forbes*

> A treasure trove of . . . fascinating deep dives into the history of travel keepsakes . . . Potts walks us through the origins of some of the most popular vacation memorabilia, including postcards and the still confoundedly ubiquitous souvenir spoons. He also examines the history of the more somber side of mementos, those depicting crimes and tragedies. Overall, the book, as do souvenirs themselves, speaks to the broader issues of time, memory, adventure, and nostalgia."
>
> *The Boston Globe*

Veil by Rafia Zakaria

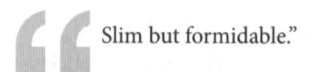

> Slim but formidable."
>
> *London Review of Books*

> Rafia Zakaria's *Veil* shifts the balance away from white secular Europe toward the experience of Muslim women, mapping the stereotypical representations of the veil in Western culture and then reflecting, in an intensely personal way, on the many meanings that the veil can have for the people who wear it . . . [*Veil* is] useful and important, providing needed insight and detail to deepen our understanding of how we got here—a necessary step for thinking about whether and how we might be able to move to a better place."
>
> *The Nation*

> An intellectually bracing, beautifully written exploration of an item of clothing all too freighted with meaning."
>
> Molly Crabapple, artist, journalist, and author of *Drawing Blood* (2015)

" The Object Lessons series achieves something very close to magic: the books take ordinary—even banal—objects and animate them with a rich history of invention, political struggle, science, and popular mythology. Filled with fascinating details and conveyed in sharp, accessible prose, the books make the everyday world come to life. Be warned: once you've read a few of these, you'll start walking around your house, picking up random objects, and musing aloud: 'I wonder what the story is behind this thing?'"

Steven Johnson, author of *Where Good Ideas Come From* and *How We Got to Now*

" Object Lessons describe themselves as 'short, beautiful books,' and to that, I'll say, amen.... If you read enough Object Lessons books, you'll fill your head with plenty of trivia to amaze and annoy your friends and loved ones—caution recommended on pontificating on the objects surrounding you. More importantly, though ... they inspire us to take a second look at parts of the everyday that we've taken for granted. These are not so much lessons about the objects themselves, but opportunities for self-reflection and storytelling. They remind us that we are surrounded by a wondrous world, as long as we care to look."

John Warner, *The Chicago Tribune*

FOAL

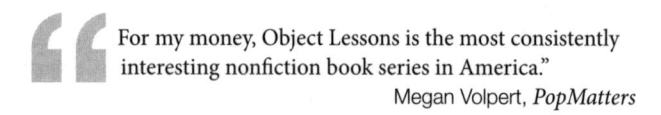

"For my money, Object Lessons is the most consistently interesting nonfiction book series in America."

Megan Volpert, *PopMatters*

"Besides being beautiful little hand-sized objects themselves, showcasing exceptional writing, the wonder of these books is that they exist at all. . . . Uniformly excellent, engaging, thought-provoking, and informative."

Jennifer Bort Yacovissi, *Washington Independent Review of Books*

". . . edifying and entertaining . . . perfect for slipping in a pocket and pulling out when life is on hold."

Sarah Murdoch, *Toronto Star*

"[W]itty, thought-provoking, and poetic. . . . These little books are a page-flipper's dream."

John Timpane, *The Philadelphia Inquirer*

"Though short, at roughly 25,000 words apiece, these books are anything but slight."

Marina Benjamin, *New Statesman*

" The joy of the series, of reading *Remote Control, Golf Ball, Driver's License, Drone, Silence, Glass, Refrigerator, Hotel,* and *Waste* . . . in quick succession, lies in encountering the various turns through which each of their authors has been put by his or her object. . . . The object predominates, sits squarely center stage, directs the action. The object decides the genre, the chronology, and the limits of the study. Accordingly, the author has to take her cue from the *thing* she chose or that chose her. The result is a wonderfully uneven series of books, each one a *thing* unto itself."

Julian Yates, *Los Angeles Review of Books*

" The Object Lessons series has a beautifully simple premise. Each book or essay centers on a specific object. This can be mundane or unexpected, humorous or politically timely. Whatever the subject, these descriptions reveal the rich worlds hidden under the surface of things."

Christine Ro, *Book Riot*

" . . . a sensibility somewhere between Roland Barthes and Wes Anderson."

Simon Reynolds, author of *Retromania: Pop Culture's Addiction to Its Own Past*